Good Luck

BRITTANE WHEELER

MW00942449

Congrats &
Good luck
♡ Mere

Good Luck!
♡ Always,
Jeanette
xo

i

# ACE LIFE EARLY

## LIFE AFTER HIGH SCHOOL

# ACE LIFE EARLY

## LIFE AFTER HIGH SCHOOL

A book that has been specifically written to teach young adults how to navigate through the important areas of life that school never told them about.

*The most asked question in high school:*

When am I ever going to use this?

*Answer:*

"I don't know, maybe never"

**Ace Life Early will teach you what your school didn't, and prepare you for what life is going to throw at you as an adult.**

Michael L. Drummond

v

# DEDICATION

To all of the young adults navigating through life's toughest challenges.

# CONTENTS

# ACKNOWLEDGMENTS

Thank you to my father for always speaking sound wisdom into my life, demonstrating financial discipline, and ensuring that I was prepared for life's challenges.

Thank you to all of the incredible people who I met while serving in the United States Marine Corps. The experiences and challenges developed me and provided an opportunity for me to mentor young adults who recently left their parent's home for the first time.

Thank you to my wonderful wife and children for always believing in and supporting me.

# ABOUT THE AUTHOR

MICHAEL L. DRUMMOND lives in North Carolina with his wife Ashley and two children, Logan and Camden. Currently he is a self-employed business owner and enjoys writing, spending time with his family, investing, riding motorcycles, golf, and going to church.

His passion for mentoring young adults stemmed from witnessing too many people make serious mistakes while navigating through the early stages of adulthood. While serving in the Marine Corps, Michael's eyes were opened to how unprepared a majority of young adults are when it comes to purchasing a vehicle, credit cards, doing their taxes, interviewing for a job, investing, and managing their money.

After graduating Summa Cum Laude with a Masters Degree in Business Administration and Finance, Michael decided that a book needed to be published that would help guide young adults through the early stages of adulthood. Michael wrote Ace Life Early so that every young adult can have access to the education that is required when starting life after high school, and to teach the important life skills that most public education institutions leave out.

# ONE

WHAT NOBODY TAUGHT YOU

Have you ever asked the question: "When am I going to use this?" Like most teenagers and young adults going through school, you have probably spent countless hours of your life learning about things such as the Pythagorean Theorem, how to properly state a hypothesis, and the correct way to read the level of liquid that is in a test tube. Schools have hired coaches and physical education teachers to show you the correct way to execute a pull-up, play soccer, or throw a football. Teachers have specifically invested time in you to ensure that you can play the recorder or create a coffee mug made out of clay.

However, the chances are that nobody at your school, an institution that is supposed to prepare you for life, has ever spent the time to teach you about interviewing for a job, credit cards, taxes, budgeting, saving for retirement, or the numerous other important events that are critical to your success as an adult.

While recognizing that some students may end up being an artist, musician, chemist, or math teacher, the truth is that a significant amount of the material being covered in high school becomes irrelevant the moment a student graduates. Sure, you need to know some basic math functions, how to properly form sentences, and enough about history to avoid looking ignorant; however, when contemplating if you are more likely to have to recite the elements contained on the periodic table, or if you will have to navigate through the process of being approved for a credit card that doesn't charge excessive fees, the answer about what is more important becomes clear.

Additionally, the consequences that are associated with making mistakes during the credit application, car buying, or job interview process could be severe, and follow you for years down the road. That's life as an adult; the decisions that you are going to have to make in the near future are going to have an impact on other areas of your life for the years to come.

Throughout this book, there will be times when subjects or topics that are routinely covered in a high school classroom may appear discredited or unimportant. I want to be clear and state that it is not my opinion that these subjects are unimportant or won't be used in the future in some capacity; but it is my opinion that the education system is leaving a large gap that results in setting teens up for failure down the road.

References that include topics such as playing the recorder or being able to properly recite the entire table of elements are simply used throughout this book to support the main topic of the book; which is that the educational system has not properly prepared you with the skills and knowledge that you will need during the early stages of adulthood, and that Ace Life Early is here to fix that problem.

Some people may think or state "it is not the school's responsibility to teach this, it is up to the student's parents." Well, the truth is that not every student lives in a household with parents who mentor them in all of these areas. In fact, some parents are struggling through the consequences of making poor decisions in the past and really don't know how to properly lead their children through these areas.

Some parents may never sit down and show their child their credit report because they are embarrassed about the contents of it, or because they simply feel that it is private information. Isn't it strange that a parent will require their child to spend a countless number of hours learning about multiple scientific theories during the years that their children are in high school, but they will not take twenty minutes to explain the differences between the two credit card offers that they receive in the mailbox every week, or how to interview for a job?

There is a time in every young adult's life when they have to realize that the system they have been a part of over the last ten to twelve years has not properly prepared them for life's most important challenges. The times of worrying about who is going to prom with who, or if the football team is going to win the state championship game is over; it is time to start preparing for life's challenges and focus in on what is truly going to be important in order for you to be successful at "adulting".

Let's focus in on some questions that will be important for you to have the answer to in the short years to come, and see where you currently stand. At what age do I need to start saving for my retirement? When am I able to contribute to an IRA? How do I file my taxes? What is the difference between a Roth and Traditional IRA? How do I properly establish credit? What is the S&P 500 and why should I care about it now? Are the credit card offers that I get in the mail when I turn eighteen a scam? What is a good interest rate when purchasing a car? How do I create a budget? How much do I need to save for retirement?

As you have probably realized while reading through that short list of questions, you have some reading to do! This book is designed to take someone through each of these topics at the most basic level. I am going to assume that you know absolutely nothing about each of the topics discussed throughout this book in order to make sure that you are not left with questions; then I will take you to a level where you feel confident about making decisions in these areas.

Sadly, there are thousands of teenagers or people in their younger twenties that make poor choices surrounding these subjects every day. Incidents such as purchasing a used vehicle with a 19% interest rate, applying for credit cards at multiple retailers throughout the local mall until one store gives approval, spending without a budget, not investing for retirement, and showing up for a job interview unprepared are examples of how thousands of teens and young adults will start heading down the wrong path at an early age.

These events that many people end up regretting down the road don't occur intentionally; they occur because nobody has specifically and purposefully invested the time to teach about these subjects. The result is that young adults making these decisions end up "winging it" or following the advice of an "*expert*" on a social media site, and all goes terribly wrong. This book is about fixing that problem and ensuring that all young adults have the opportunity to head down the correct path from the beginning. Let's dive in!

# TWO

APPLYING FOR A JOB

Getting a good paying job is difficult in today's workplace. Economic recessions and other factors have caused large quantities of experienced adult workers to seek employment in fields that have traditionally been filled by teens or young adults in the past. What does this mean for you? It means that you have to step up your game and get prepared to fight for the job that you want.

Employers are bombarded with multiple applications every week; why should they choose you? I will answer that question by ensuring that you are properly prepared for every step of the job application and interview process.

First, it is important for you to realize that the job interview process starts the moment that you pull into the parking lot to ask for an application. For example, what is the manager, who happened to be walking in from their lunch break while you were walking through the parking lot, going to think about the gum wrapper that you threw on the ground while walking in?

Always go in with the mindset that you are being evaluated from the moment your car's tires touch the parking lot, until you are completely out of sight. Leave nothing up to chance and make a purposeful attempt to be polite to everyone you meet; you never know who they are.

One of the most common mistakes that young adults make when applying for a job is thinking that the task of picking up an application is not important, or that they don't have to dress professionally for that moment because it is not a "job interview". In reality, the person giving you the application to fill out is most likely considering if they are going to give it to their manager, or if it is going to go straight into the recycling bin after you leave. Remember, you are always being evaluated! This is not the time to wear your cut off shorts, tank top, politically incorrect shirt, leggings, or yoga pants; this is the time to show that you are the professional that this company would like to trust with its reputation and loyal customer base.

Let's start from the beginning and walk through this process together. As an example throughout this chapter, we will fictitiously apply for a job at a major electronic retail store, and in this scenario the store has an opening for a full-time employee in the computer department.

The first step that you need to take is to conduct a small amount of research about the company and available positions. Start out with visiting the company's website if it has one, and by conducting an online search about the history of the company. Not only will this process give you a little bit of information about the place that you are going to spend hours of your life at, but it will also give you the opportunity to impress your interviewer later on in the employment selection process, which I will highlight later in this chapter.

What information should you specifically focus on? Start out with trying to find out the name of the store manager and the supervisor of the department that you are going to apply for. Next, read into the company's community relations activities. Many corporations donate money or sponsor specific events that coincide with the industry they are in. For instance, the electronic retail store you are applying at, may award scholarships to college students who are studying for degrees in technology fields. Lastly, learn about the culture of the company, the position's requirements, and average pay for the position in the industry in accordance with your geographical location.

Let's pause momentarily to answer the question that was asked in the beginning of this book, and is asked throughout high school by most students: When am I ever going to use this?

Knowing the store manager's name will afford you the opportunity to know who you are speaking with, and what stage of the interview process that you may be in. Don't be surprised if you are asked to complete more than one job interview. It is common for a departmental manager or supervisor to conduct preliminary interviews to weed out unqualified applicants; this prevents the store manager, or upper management level personnel, from wasting their time dealing with the yoga pants wearing, gum chomping, cigarette smelling, unprepared applicants.

Now that you know a little bit about the company that you are going to apply at, it is time to work on the information that the company will find out about you. A great place to start is with all social media websites or groups that you belong to. Believe it or not, one of the first things that many hiring managers will do when they receive an application, is conduct an online search so that they can see anything that is available through your social media footprint.

Although most people understand that social media can be a place to share funny pictures, posts filled with satire, and information pertaining to how your day is going, it is highly recommended that people applying for jobs scrub their social media profiles, and get rid of anything that could make them look unprofessional or unfit for employment.

Posts on social media that are overly political, suggestive of drug use, have pictures of people doing keg stands, and complain about a prior employer will not help you get a job. The defense "this is my page and I should be able to post what I want" is no longer acceptable; you are an adult, and employers don't want to hear or see it.

If your social media profile is filled with a long history of posts and pictures that you would prefer your future employer not to see, I suggest temporarily disabling your profile until you are done with your job search.

The next task that you have to complete before going into the store to request a job application is to write a resume. Although your resume may not be filled with years of experience and a long job history, due to your age or the current stage of life that you are in, creating a resume shows employers that you are a professional and are serious about working for their company. Volunteer work and any type of academic recognition are great ways to fill the void of experience that is common among teens and young adults searching for employment.

If you are not familiar with creating a resume, I recommend using one of the many free online resume builder websites that can be found through a quick online search; this will ensure that you have a resume that is professional in appearance and formatted correctly.

Most likely, the online resume builder will provide you with the option to choose between a "functional" or a "chronological" resume format. If you do not have a significant amount of work history, but have skills that you would like to highlight, a functional resume would work best. In contrast, if you have held a few jobs in the past and are looking to include that experience in your resume, a chronological resume format will likely be your best option.

The correct choice between these two formats is the one that will quickly and clearly highlight your experience; remember, the person looking through resumes has hundreds to go through and does not want to read an essay written by you and about you. In most cases, teens and young adults should be able to fit their entire resume onto a single page.

Ensure that you include two or three references on your resume; these should consist of prior employers, a community leader, teacher, or coach and all of your references should be aware that they are being listed. Don't simply assume that your references are going to speak highly about you, make sure to have a discussion with each person and ask them what they are able or willing to say. Be aware that prior employers may not be able to say much about you, other than verifying your dates of employment, due to their company's rules and regulations, or employment laws.

Once your resume is complete, you need to prepare yourself for picking up the job application at the store. Although you have probably been told numerous times throughout your life not to judge someone by their appearance, this is exactly what is going to happen to you throughout your job seeking experience.

Looking professional does not mean that you have to rent a tuxedo or wear a full suit; it simply means that you are dressed according to the industry's standards. For the position at the electronics store in our scenario, the appropriate attire would be khaki pants with a nice pair of shoes and a polo shirt.

Women who desire to wear a skirt should ensure that the skirt is long enough to touch the top of their knees and looks professional. Additionally, low-cut or revealing shirts should be avoided to ensure that you have a professional appearance and do not send out the wrong signals.

After getting dressed, ensure that all other hygiene steps are taken. If the person giving you the application or your interviewer notices that you have dirty fingernails, bad breath, and body odor, it is likely that they will not be overly thrilled with the thought of having to be around you every day, or the idea of you dealing with their customers.

Don't go overboard on the cologne or perfume, as this is a turn-off as well; your goal is to present yourself in a manner that people will not remember anything negative about. If the employees in the store are talking about your cologne or the way you smell once you leave, it is a bad thing.

If you use tobacco, do not do it prior to picking up an application or a job interview. Many people are turned off by smokers and people who use chewing tobacco. Additionally, it is important to remember that managers are seeking to hire an employee who is going to be productive; when you show up smelling like cigarette smoke, the manager might be thinking about all of the five to seven minute smoke breaks that you are going to take throughout the day. The fact that you smoke will not get you hired, so this is not something that you want your interviewer to place any focus on, or to be thinking about.

Many people who deal with the public daily also find it rude to chew gum while having a conversation. Constant chewing can be distracting to others, so if you are worried about your breath eat a small mint prior to walking inside.

The last step that you need to take prior to going into the store to ask for an application is to ensure that you have something to write with and the personal documents that you may need for the application. Carrying a pen shows that you are prepared, and prevents you from having to interrupt an employee to ask for one. Also, remember that the job application may require you to provide some personal information, such as your driver's license number, social security number, and information about prior employers; make sure that you have this information with you in case the person giving you the application instructs you to complete it while at the store.

Ensure that your cell phone or any other type of electronic device is turned off. You do not want anything to interrupt your conversation with a manager, or to make the person who you are talking with feel unimportant.

When asking for the application, ensure that you do not interrupt the employee from doing their job! Be patient and wait for a time when the employee is not busy to ask for the application.

Since you have done your homework, you already know that the store is looking to hire a full-time employee in its computer department. Approach the employee at the customer service desk with a friendly greeting, and request an application.

If the employee simply hands the application to you, and does not provide any instructions for how or where to fill it out, it is appropriate to take it home or to another location and return it later. However, if the employee provides any instructions when handing you the application, follow their directions precisely. Take your time when filling out the application and write legibly; this application may be the first item that a manager sees associated with your name, so make sure it represents you well. Ensure to fill out the application completely, and follow all of the directions; missing steps or filling out something incorrectly may send a signal that you have difficulty following directions.

After filling out the application, return it to the appropriate person, along with your resume, and thank them for their time. Remain professional and as if you are being evaluated until you are completely out of sight and off of the company's property.

Allow five to seven days for a store associate to contact you about your application. If you are not contacted within this time period, follow up with a phone call. Ensure that you do not appear "pushy" when asking about your application, but that you are very interested in working for the company.

Most likely, a manager is going to call you, and ask you to come in for an interview. Since you know that this is a possibility, make sure that your voicemail message is professional and friendly, in case the call comes at a time when you are unavailable or can't pick up the phone. The last thing that you want the person calling you to come in for an interview to hear, is obscene music being played as your phone rings or a voicemail message that could leave an impression that you are immature.

When you pick up the phone, ensure to speak clearly, greet the person calling, and immediately move to a location that is quiet for the remainder of the phone call. Remember the person's name who you are speaking with, tell them that you look forward to meeting with them, confirm the interview location, time, date, and say thank you prior to ending the conversation.

## THE INTERVIEW

Now that you have an interview scheduled with a manager for the job that you applied for, it is time to prepare for this stage of the employment selection process.

The job interview is what is going to make or break your chances of getting hired at the job you want. All of the steps that you took in order to get to this point, such as not smoking prior to the interview, having a professional appearance, and bringing a pen, matter even more during this stage of the employment selection process.

The first event that is going to occur during the interview, and one that will leave a very lasting impression, is that you are going to have to introduce yourself to the person who is going to interview you.

Make sure that you smile, look the person in the eyes, extend a firm handshake, and politely introduce yourself. The way that you shake someone's hand is important as well. Nobody likes the "dead fish" handshake; this is where someone shakes your hand so lightly that if feels like you are holding a dead fish, or simply holding hands. Also, this is not a time where you are attempting to show dominance or how much strength you have, so you squeeze the interviewer's hand so hard that it is uncomfortable for them. The handshake you give should simply be firm and completely interlocked; don't just grab their fingers or tip of their hand, fully press into the handshake so that your thumb and index fingers interlock with theirs.

Additionally, if your interviewer is a female, do not shake their hand any different than you would a male's. You are in the workplace in a professional environment, and everyone should be treated equally and professionally. Shaking a female manager's hand differently than a male's hand, will likely come off as offensive and will not increase your chances of getting the job.

Now that you have properly introduced yourself, it is likely that your interviewer will begin with asking you a few questions. The first thing to know is that there are a few very common questions that are asked in almost every job interview. Taking some time to research common job interview questions, and thinking about how you are going to answer these questions during the interview, will make you more prepared and will calm your nerves. Let's go over a few questions that you are likely to get, and talk about ways to answer them.

First, the interviewer is likely to ask you to tell them a little bit about yourself. When this question is asked, understand that the interviewer is not necessarily interested in hearing about your mom, three sisters, and dog, but is looking to gain insight into what you are passionate about or what drives you to succeed.

An appropriate answer to this question in the scenario given for this chapter would be: "I am really passionate about developing technology and learning more about electronics; I spend a lot of time with my family or working on computers, because this is the field that I want to have a career in."

This answer gives the interviewer a little bit of insight into what you are passionate about, while also telling them how you spend your free time, that you enjoy your family, and that you are goal oriented in regards to what you want to do in the future.

Another question that you are likely to get during an interview is: What would you say is your greatest weakness? This question is often asked by interviewers because they want to see how you handle stress, and if you are willing to admit that you have a weakness. Replying with "I don't know" or "I really don't think I have one in regards to this job's requirements" will tell the interviewer that you may be difficult to train or mentor; because you think that you don't have faults or areas where you can improve.

When replying to this question, you want to admit a weakness that can also show strength. For instance, "I think that my greatest weakness is that I have trouble handing over control of things that I am responsible for to others; sometimes I have difficulty trusting others with tasks, because I am afraid they will not do it to the same standards or as efficiently as I would." This response answers the interviewer's original question, but also leaves them with the impression that you care about quality, efficiency, and getting the job done correctly. If there is room for more conversation, you could add that you realize this is an area where you need to improve, because you believe in teamwork and realize the importance of trusting your peers and co-workers.

Next, your interviewer may ask "why do you want to work for this company?" This is a perfect opportunity to show off how prepared you are for this job interview, and how you are different from the other people who are interviewing for this position.

An answer that you can give to this question is "I have always been passionate about working with computers and technology, I have enjoyed being a customer at this store, and I really envy this company's decision to give back to the community by extending college scholarships to young adults who are furthering their education in a technology field; I am confident that I would really enjoy coming to work every day at this company."

This question is one of the reasons why doing your research in the beginning is important. Your answer to this question informed your interviewer that you are passionate about the products that you will be dealing with, but most importantly it showed that you conducted research, went the extra mile to learn about the company, care about this job position, and are taking this interview seriously.

After providing an answer such as this, it will be very evident to your interviewer that you did not simply walk around a shopping complex to fill out a bunch of applications one day, but that you specifically targeted this business because it is the place that you really want to work at. This is guaranteed to make the person interviewing you feel as though they did not waste their time calling you in for an interview.

Finally, you may get asked the question "out of all of the other people applying for this job, why should we hire you?" When responding to this question, your goal should be to provide an answer that will give your interviewer confidence in their decision to hire you; understand that your interviewer is also accountable for the decisions that they make, and they want to ensure that they will be able to take pride in their decision to hire you, instead of regretting it and possibly losing the confidence of higher management to make staffing decisions in the future.

Answer this question with confidence, look your interviewer in the eyes and reply with an answer such as "You should hire me because I can promise you that I will be 100% committed to the goals of your department, because I am punctual, professional, and will always come to work with a positive attitude, eager to learn, and looking to improve your department and customers' overall experience. I can promise you that I will always give you my best work, that I truly care about this company, and that I will strive to be the best employee that you have ever had."

A statement like the one listed above will only work and make an impact with your interviewer if it is stated with confidence, and if your interviewer believes you. If you showed up to the interview a few minutes late, unprepared, and appeared unprofessional, your statement will not be impactful. This is another reason why researching the company prior to the interview is a critical step; you can use the information gained through your research to build a trusting relationship throughout the interview, which will enable you to leave an unforgettable and favorable impression in the end.

Another area that you should be prepared to speak about during the job interview is how much you would like to get paid. It is not uncommon for interviewers to bring this topic up around the conclusion of the interview, especially if they are strongly considering you for employment.

If the interviewer asks you how much money you expect to be paid, you should be able to respond with an answer such as "I have conducted some research into what the average pay for someone with my experience is throughout this industry, and think that (insert relevant amount of money) is fair."

You should be able to make this statement with confidence because you paid attention to the beginning of this chapter, and did your research on the average pay for someone with your experience, in the geographical area for the position that you are applying for.

This answer will continue to increase your credibility with the interviewer, and will ensure that you are only asking for what is fair and considered as the industry standard. Mentioning a dollar amount that is significantly out of alignment with the industry standard will make you appear uninformed and unrealistic.

Your interview will likely end with a job offer, or a handshake and a statement letting you know that they will be in touch soon.

If you receive a job offer, make sure to say thank you, and show that you are excited for the future. If you have questions about the position, benefits, opportunities for advancement in the future, hours, travel, employment requirements, or anything else, this is the time to ask those questions.

Ensure that you don't get caught up in the moment of landing the job and forget to ask what your next steps are. Many companies will require you to take a drug test within a 24-hour period of being offered a job, or to fill out additional paperwork; make sure to write down the specifics of the steps that you need to take, and complete everything as instructed.

If you don't receive an immediate job offer, but are told by the interviewer that they will contact you in the future, realize that this is simply the way some companies conduct their hiring process. Make sure to thank the interviewer for their time, shake their hand, and tell them that you are looking forward to hearing from them soon.

If you do not receive a call back within the next 4-5 business days, follow up with a phone call to the manager that you had the interview with and ask if they have made a decision pertaining to the position that you applied for. If the manager responds with "we are still conducting interviews and have not made a decision yet", simply acknowledge their response, thank them for their time, and end the conversation by stating that you look forward to hearing from them soon.

A response that you may also receive is that the company decided to fill the position with someone other than you, meaning that you did not get the job.

Although this is surely not the response that you were looking for, you need to view this as a learning opportunity. You have nothing to lose by simply leveling with the person who interviewed you, and requesting their constructive criticism. Politely ask the interviewer "if you don't mind, could you please tell me something that you feel I could have done better while applying for the position at your company?" Another question to ask is if there is a tangible qualification that you are missing, or something else that you can complete to make you more sought after by companies throughout the industry.

Realize that finding the right job in the career path that you desire is often times a journey. The most important step in the process of getting the job you want usually revolves around preparation and research. If you truly prepare for every step of the job application process, you will likely be more confident and less nervous.

A few key points that you need to take away from this chapter are preparation is key, appearance is important, and that the job interview starts the minute that your car's tires hit the parking lot. Also, don't ever discount the value of a good smile and a firm handshake.

# THREE

## CREATING A BUDGET THAT WORKS

One of the hardest parts of managing the responsibilities that will be thrown at you after graduating high school, or starting to live on your own, is keeping track of your money. With debit cards, credit cards, and mobile payment applications being used as the primary methods for payment, it is easier than ever for a person to lose track of how much money they have in their account. Overdraft protection allows shoppers to continue purchasing without the proper funds available; this is permitted by banks because they enjoy profiting from the fees that they charge you when this occurs. It is too easy to simply swipe your card, and not have to feel the repercussions of a poor decision instantaneously.

Before reading this chapter and creating your budget, you need to recognize that this process takes discipline, honesty, courage, and humility. The most important characteristics about a "budget that works for you" are that the budget has to be organized and realistic. If you cannot lay out all of your finances in an organized manner, and be honest with how much money you are accustomed to spending on different items, your budget will not stand the test of time.

Throughout this process, take note that we are not going to list specific percentages of your paycheck that should be designated towards certain areas of your life, other than saving 10% of what you make. For instance, some financial experts will specify that you should spend no more than 30% of your income on your mortgage, or less than 20% of your income on automobile expenses.

I will not state a specific percentage for certain expenses because I believe doing this sets people up for failure. Telling someone to set aside a specific percentage of their paycheck, for something that is not that important of an item to them, is not a part of "creating a budget that works for you" and will likely breed disappointment in the early stages. People who have religious beliefs that call for them to tithe 10% of their earnings will have a different looking budget than someone who does not share in this belief; a budget cannot be a one size fits all solution, and has to be structured in a way that gives priority to your specific interests and circumstances.

This is your budget, and it is supposed to be designed towards your lifestyle. The fact is that everyone has different priorities, interests, hobbies, and things that they work hard for in order to be able to afford. It is usually easy to tell what is important to someone by looking at their bank statement; if someone really cares about expensive jewelry, their bank statement will reflect that a significant amount of their money goes towards expensive jewelry, and this will remain true with hobbies such as golf, a nice house, expensive cars, fancy clothing, or commitment to their church. Your bank statement is the biggest tattle-tale that your heart will ever face; it shows what you truly desire, love, and value.

This does not mean that I recommend spending 80% of your money on cars because it is what you care about most; it simply means that everyone has different interests, and therefore everyone's plan for their money should be different.

Although everyone's budget is going to look different, and reflect different situations that are specific to their life, there is one area that should share some commonality, and that is designating a portion of income towards savings and retirement.

Regardless of if you are interested in cars, jewelry, traveling, or video games, the fact is that there will come a point in your life when you are going to have to rely on the money that you stocked away in a savings or retirement account in the past.

One thing that will become evident during the early stages of adulthood is that there is always something that needs to be paid for. Most of the time, the air conditioning going out in your car, tire that blows, or tooth ache that needs to be taken care of immediately is not something that is planned for, but it can and should be through the emergency fund that you maintain.

Something to keep in mind while you are creating your budget is that it is supposed to be a detailed and very meticulous plan for where you are telling your money to go. You should refuse to be one of the people who look at their bank account, and are surprised by where all of their money went or how much they spent. Absolutely refuse to allow this to ever happen to you; you tell your money where to go! Let's get started on creating a budget that is going to work for you.

The first step in creating a "budget that works for you" is to print out the last 3 months of bank statements that you have, and to gather every bill that you are required to pay in the future. Going through your bank statements and evaluating every expense is a tedious process, but is a necessary step in order for you to gain a clear understanding of how you spend your money each month.

Using a Microsoft Excel spreadsheet, create categories for each expense that you have, and separate them by month. For instance, if you are evaluating the months of January, February, and March, you should have a category titled "groceries" and there should be separate boxes on the spreadsheet to input each month's expense.

Other common categories that you can create in order to ensure that your budget is organized are: Insurance, automobile expenses, credit card payments, dining out, clothes, medical expenses, household utilities, gifts, cell phones, entertainment, and rent or mortgage payment. Simply go through each line on your bank statement and create a category for each expense that you have; these categories should be specific enough that they will accurately define the expense, but broad enough so that you don't end up with hundreds of categories. An example of this would be labeling a category as "household utilities", and recording all of your electric, water, and garbage bills under the same category.

An important category to create is one titled "non-essentials". This category is where you should place the random or spontaneous convenience store purchases, such as a pack of gum, energy drink, tobacco products, bag of chips, or extra cup of coffee that you purchased, but didn't really need or plan for.

It is important to separate these types of items and label them as non-essential instead of including them into a category such as "groceries" because it will allow you to see how quickly these small purchases add up, and will afford you the opportunity to see where you can make some cuts in your spending if you don't have enough income to cover all of your expenses. Most of the time, this category will be the most eye-opening experience of the entire budget creating process, and will result in you saying "I can't believe I spend that much on (fill in the blank) each month."

After you finish creating a category for each expense that you have on your bank statement, think about any other expense that you pay for using cash, or that would not be included on your bank statement, and create the necessary category for it.

Now that all of your categories are completed and organized on a Microsoft Excel spreadsheet so that it is easy to view and insert information, you need to insert your expenses into each category on the spreadsheet that you completed. I find it easiest to pick a category and then go through the monthly statement line by line, adding each expense together for that category on a calculator, and placing a check mark next to the item on the statement to depict that it has already been accounted for. Record the monthly total for each category under the appropriate month on the spreadsheet. Repeat this process for each of the three months until you have every expense on your statement inputted into your spreadsheet and accounted for.

After every expense and bill that you have to pay is recorded by category and month, it is time to evaluate the information and find out what the average amount that you spend per month is for each category.

There are a few different ways that you can find the average of your expenses. If you are not familiar with Microsoft Excel or using the function key to create formulas, you can simply click and highlight the cells that contain the information that you would like to find the average of, and it will be displayed automatically in the bottom right section of the spreadsheet.

If you would like to create a formula using the function key, click on the cell where you would like the average to be displayed at, then click the "insert function" icon that looks like "*fx*", select "average" from the dropdown menu, click "ok", highlight the cells that contain the numbers you would like to calculate an average for, then click "ok". The average will appear and will automatically be adjusted if you edit the data in the cells that were selected during the creation of the formula.

Example 3.1

| Category | Jan | Feb | Mar | Average |
|----------|---------|---------|---------|---------|
| Groceries | 237.65 | 287.54 | 254.44 | 259.88 |
| Gas | 87.65 | 95.55 | 155.60 | 112.93 |
| Rent | 950.00 | 950.00 | 950.00 | 950.00 |
| Total | 1275.30 | 1333.09 | 1360.04 | 1322.81 |

Lastly, create a section on your spreadsheet for annual expenses; this section is for items such as your vehicle registration or a subscription that is due once per year. Ensure that you put the date that you will have to pay this bill on the spreadsheet so that you can properly prepare for the expense as it gets closer and doesn't come as a surprise.

Now that you have an average for what you spend, it is time to look at your income and determine how much you can actually afford. Start out by labeling a section on your spreadsheet titled "Income".

If you get paid a salary, meaning that your paycheck is the same amount each pay period, simply insert your monthly amount under "Income". If your paychecks vary, or you work in a career field such as a waiter or waitress where the amount that you get paid is different each day, you will need to do some work by going through each of your pay stubs or records to get the most accurate number as possible for your monthly income.

Next, subtract your total monthly expenses from your total income. Hopefully this number is positive and you are making more than you spend each month. Unfortunately, many Americans find themselves outspending their income every month and falling further and further into debt. Data collected in 2016 showed that the average American household had $16,061 in credit card debt; this number is 10% higher than it was in 2006, and does not include debt such as personal, student, and automobile loans. We will dive deeper into credit cards and how detrimental this type of debt is to your financial future later on in the chapter titled "Establishing Credit and Credit Cards".

Now that you have an accurate picture of what your financial status is, it is time to lay out some ground rules and determine what you're going to budget for each category during every month going forward. During this process, you need to be honest with yourself and set realistic but necessary goals.

For each category, set a percentage or amount of your income that you are going to spend each month.

Regardless of how much money you make, or if you have a surplus of income, it is important to have a plan for each dollar that you make and to stick to a spending plan. An example of people not doing this, are the professional athletes that made millions of dollars every year, but go broke after being out of the sports world for a few years; this occurs because they failed to create a budget, or stick to a disciplined spending plan.

As mentioned earlier on in this chapter, you need to save a minimum of 10% of your income each month. Make transferring the money from your checking account to your savings or retirement account the very first thing that you do every time you get paid. Treat this as if it is the most important bill that you have, because it is!

Most likely, if you choose to wait and transfer the money to your savings or retirement account at the end of the month, you will end up spending more on non-essential items, and selling yourself short when it comes to saving for the future.

The Federal Reserve Board stated in recent studies that over 50% of Americans would need to sell something or use a credit card to cover an unexpected expense greater than $400; let's not ever fall into this statistic!

Additionally, you need to make a rule for when you are going to spend money that you have in savings. It is not okay to overspend your budgeted amount throughout the month, and then transfer $50 from your savings account because you want to go out to the movies with friends; this is when you have to say "it is not in my budget right now, I can't go".

Your savings should only be used for emergencies and specific purchases that you are directly saving for. Also, create a non-negotiable amount that you will keep in your savings account as an emergency fund; this is used for when your only vehicle's tire blows, or when you have to pay for unexpected medical expenses and you have absolutely no choice but to take money out of your savings account.

After you have determined how much you are going to put towards saving each month, the next step is to look at the areas of your spending that you have the power to change, and set an amount that you are going to budget for each category. While doing this, you may find out that you need to change the way you act or live.

Outspending what you make every month or not meeting your savings goals cannot be acceptable to you! Using a credit card for expenses that you cannot afford, and then only paying the minimum balance due at the end of the month, is going to make your financial situation worse, and push you further into debt down the road. Before you know it, all of the $4 café lattes that you purchased on your credit card over the past few months are still not paid for, and are accumulating interest.

Closely evaluate the "non-essential" category that you created and make a resolution to eliminate items that are keeping you from reaching your goals.

If you still don't have enough money, or are not satisfied with how much you spend in a certain area, ways that you can lower some of your bills are to cut out unnecessary driving, alter your cable, internet, or phone package, eat out less, and grocery shop with your budget in mind. Sometimes, drastic changes such as where you live, the car you drive, or food that you eat needs to be adjusted in order to make your budget work. If you wait to make these changes because they are uncomfortable, difficult, or inconvenient, it is only going to be harder to correct your financial situation in the future; identify past mistakes, make corrections quickly, and move forward.

Recognize that the budget you created will change often, and that you need to constantly track what you're spending each week to ensure that you are staying within the amount that you set to spend on each category. The days of buying something simply because you have enough money in your checking account at that time are over; plan, save, and spend intelligently.

As your life changes, so should your budget. Prior to making a purchase, such as a new automobile, you need to see if the purchase is going to fit in your budget; if the purchase is going to result in you not being able to save, then don't make the purchase.

Only making purchases that fit your budget will save you from a lot of stress, anxiety, and sleepless nights in the future. Set milestone goals for your savings account, and reward yourself with a small treat when you accomplish a goal. Over time, you will learn to find more joy in looking at your bank account, than you used to when looking at a new pair of shoes that you just bought!

Although major life changes such as marriage, having children, or purchasing your first home may not be on your mind right now, it is a critical to develop sound budgeting and spending practices early on in life, so that you will be fully prepared when life's challenges hit you. Create a habit of following a budget early on in life, and it will be easier for you to do when you have a family, more bills, and emergencies that are of higher importance.

# FOUR

BUYING A CAR

Before we dive in, I would like to share with you that the topic discussed in this chapter is one of the main reasons for why Ace Life Early was written. When I was on active duty in the Marine Corps, I was in charge of a significant number of young adults, who recently left their parent's home for the first time, and had to navigate through the process of purchasing a car for the very first time.

One of the things that I witnessed most, and tried to prevent during the years I spent leading younger United States Marines, was a 19 or 20 year old purchasing a ten year old car, with a 19% interest rate, at an unreasonable price, with no warranty, and a six year loan. The young man or woman had no clue how much insurance was going to cost for the car prior to signing the paperwork, which meant that they didn't even know if they could afford what they just signed their name to. If this doesn't sound like a horrible situation to be in, listen up because you have a lot to gain from this chapter!

Why does the scenario described above occur? The answer isn't because the young adult is dumb or careless; the answer is because nobody along the way took the time to educate them on the subject of how to purchase or lease a car. Ace Life Early was written to ensure that you are prepared to handle this challenge; much more, so that you can be a mentor to others who are going through this same challenge, and prevent them from making costly mistakes. Let's dive in!

First, purchasing a vehicle is an exciting experience, for those who understand the process that is going to occur at the dealership. For someone who is uneducated about the car buying process, this can be a very stressful event and result in years of regret or buyer's remorse.

Everyone wants to get a good deal when they buy a new or used car, but how do you know if you are getting a good deal or not? Is there a way to ensure that you will not have buyer's remorse a few weeks or months after making the purchase?

This chapter is dedicated to preparing you for what is going to be thrown at you when searching for your next vehicle, and throughout the entire car buying process.

Some of the questions that are going to be covered in this chapter are: Is this the right car for me? What are the steps that I need to take if I am going to purchase a used vehicle from a friend or someone on the internet? Is the interest rate that I am getting from the dealership appropriate for my current financial situation? Should I lease a vehicle? Should I purchase the warranty that the finance office is trying to sell me? What is "Gap Insurance" and should I get it? Has this vehicle ever been in a bad collision or other type of accident? Can I afford this vehicle?

These are all questions that if left unanswered can lead to buyer's remorse or some form of regret down the road. Regardless of how great the features of the car are, how much you like the color, or how nice of a person you thought that the sales person was throughout the transaction, the real judgment of how well you did while purchasing an automobile occurs when the bill is due, or when something unexpected happens.

Just as we did in the prior chapters, we are going to break down the task of searching for and purchasing a car into a step-by-step process that ensures you fully understand every aspect of the car buying experience, and feel prepared to do so with confidence.

Step one in the car buying process starts much like any other important decision that you have to make in life, with self-evaluation and research. In regards to self-evaluation, this means that you need to take an honest look at how you use your car, how that may change over the next five years, specific features and capabilities that you need your vehicle to have, and what you can afford.

The goal of the car buying process that we are going to follow throughout this chapter is to purchase a vehicle that meets your needs and is within your budget, not simply purchasing a vehicle that you want. Keep in mind that we are not concerned with personal image, social class associated with luxury brands, or appearance, but that the goal is to ensure that you make a financially sound and responsible purchase of an automobile that will fit your needs for a reasonable and foreseeable time period. Because of the demographic that this book is directed towards, we are not going to discuss options of purchasing a new sports car with an $80,000 price tag attached to it.

When looking at the types of cars and evaluating your needs, take note that there are not hundreds of long-bed pickup trucks driving around New York City; this isn't because people living there don't like long-bed pickup trucks, it is because it is nearly impossible to park this type of vehicle anywhere in New York City. In contrast, the farmers in Indiana and ranchers in Montana are not driving hybrid 4-cylinders without towing or hauling capacity. These examples are true because people in these areas evaluated their circumstances, completed a self-evaluation, and purchased a vehicle that fits their lifestyle and needs.

Simply put, you need to conduct a self-evaluation that highlights what you truly need from your vehicle, and use this evaluation to point you in the right direction when starting your research and the car buying process.

A great way to start the self-evaluation process is to write down where you go and what type of activities that you use your vehicle for. Some factors to consider during this part of the evaluation are distance traveled, road and weather conditions, parking availability, seating capabilities, and towing requirements.

After performing this part of the self-evaluation, you should be able to determine what style or type of vehicle will best suit your current needs, such as a truck, economy car, or sport utility vehicle.

When analyzing the factors that you wrote down during this part of the evaluation, also consider the importance of each factor, and other options available for you to meet rare needs that require your vehicle to have certain features. For example, if you have only used your vehicle to tow a trailer twice within the past year, it may be more appropriate to simply rent a truck that is capable of towing during those times, instead of paying the additional costs all year that come with owning a truck.

Also, it is important to think about how your life is going to change over the next five years. A five year period is appropriate because this parallels the time period of most automobile loans; this will ensure that you don't get stuck paying for a vehicle that no longer meets your needs due to predictable changes in your life.

Are you going to move locations where the weather is severely different? Are you in a serious relationship or engaged to be married? Are you about to start college in another state and plan to commute to your hometown to visit friends and family once per month?

A concept to keep in mind during the self-evaluation process is that your circumstances should determine the type of vehicle you have, instead of allowing for the type of vehicle that you have to determine your circumstances. The vehicle that you purchase is supposed to make your life easier and assist you, not hinder your lifestyle.

Now that you have evaluated your lifestyle, and determined which type or style of vehicle best fits your needs, it is time to reflect on what you can afford. Remember, just because you currently make enough money to pay the amount that is due every month for a vehicle, it does not mean that the price is going to align with the budget that you created earlier; this may mean that you cannot afford the vehicle that you want right now in the future.

I have heard many people make comments such as "if I quit smoking I can afford this car" or "I'm not going to get a cappuccino or energy drink every day on the way to work anymore, and then I can use the money that I save to pay for this car".

This type of thinking is extremely irresponsible and will likely get you into financial trouble! Look at your budget and decide how much you are able to afford to put towards a vehicle, while still meeting the other lifestyle goals that you have identified as important, such as saving for retirement, tithing, and a yearly vacation with your family.

If you sacrifice these goals in order to get a more expensive car, there is a greater chance of you experiencing buyer's remorse and regretting your decision in the future. Remember from the previous chapter, your budget is not based off of random percentages that someone else set for you or suggested, but in accordance with what you identified as what is most important to you; therefore, don't sacrifice what you have already deemed as more important simply because you are excited about a new vehicle and get caught up in the moment.

After an honest self-evaluation has been conducted, you are ready to begin researching the type of vehicle that is going to best meet your needs. Research always starts with looking at what you need the most first. For instance, if you are most concerned with fuel efficiency, then you should start conducting research to find out which model vehicles offer the best fuel range. If towing capability, suspension that can handle rough terrain, or vehicles that perform well in snow or icy conditions are major concerns of yours, then you should start searching online and recording which vehicles perform best in these different areas.

Sadly, the mistake that most people make is simply saying "I need a new vehicle and I really want to get a truck", and then they bounce around from dealership to dealership looking at different trucks until they find one they like. The problem with this process is that you are more likely to end up with something that doesn't meet some of your most important needs, and then regretting the decision shortly after the purchase.

While conducting your initial research, try to narrow your options down to five specific vehicles that you feel will meet all of your needs; then, try to factor in price and narrow your search to two or three vehicles that best align with your budget and needs.

After having two or three specific vehicles in mind, conduct an online search within a 100 mile radius of your location for that specific vehicle. Pay attention to the mileage, price, and condition of the vehicles being sold in your area. This step is important because it will help you understand the price that other dealerships or people in your area are selling these vehicles for.

Researching what a fair price is for a vehicle that you have decided upon is an important step. Don't simply go into a dealership or somewhere to look at cars without knowing what a vehicle is actually worth or being sold for at other dealerships. The price that is on the sticker at one dealership is of little concern to you; the important number is what the vehicle is actually worth, and what you are willing to pay.

A great resource that you can use while researching what the cars on your list are worth is Kelly Blue Book's website. On this website, you have the ability to input all of the features of a vehicle that you would like to purchase, select the vehicle's condition and mileage, and view what the vehicle is worth in a private party sale or at a dealership.

Another step to take while evaluating the price of a vehicle is to look at how the vehicle depreciates over time. Some vehicles lose their value faster than others, and this will have a significant impact on what the vehicle will be worth when you want to sell it in the future. To see how the vehicles that you are looking at depreciate, look at the difference in what dealerships are selling the vehicle for when it is new, and then conduct some online searches for the same car using prior year models. If a vehicle sells for $20,000 new, but is only worth $12,000 on Kelly Blue Book's website two years later, this means that the vehicle does not hold its value very well. Of course, this strategy will only apply to purchasing used vehicles, but specific manufacturers or brands do tend to have similar depreciation percentages over the years.

After finding out what the vehicles that you're looking at are worth, print any information that you have so that you can use it during the price negotiation process at the dealership (which we will get into in a little bit).

Another area that you have to research and keep in mind when looking into what you can afford is the cost of insuring the vehicle. All financing companies require that you carry "full coverage" on a vehicle that you purchase with a loan, instead of buying the car outright with cash or a check.

The term "full coverage" is widely used in the insurance industry and at car dealerships, but is not the actual name of a policy that is available for purchase. "Full coverage" is understood as an insurance policy that includes liability, collision, and comprehensive insurance. Liability insurance is required by law of all drivers, and its purpose is to cover damage to property or injuries that you may cause to someone else during an automotive accident. Collision insurance pays for damages that occur to your vehicle during an accident. Comprehensive insurance is designed to cover incidents that are not the result of a collision, such as vandalism or theft.

Before going to the dealership to look at the vehicles that you have on your list, it is a good idea to call your insurance company and request a quote for the vehicles that you are looking at. Without the Vehicle Identification Number (VIN), the insurance company will not be able to provide you with an exact insurance quote, but it will be relatively close and will allow you to understand if the cost of insurance is something that you can afford or not.

If you are not financing the vehicle, it is up to you if you only want to purchase liability insurance, or if you would also like to include collision and comprehensive. While making this decision, think about how much the car is worth and what the difference in price is for each policy; also, consider how your finances or lifestyle would be impacted if the vehicle was stolen or in a serious collision, and you did not receive any money from the insurance company to purchase another vehicle.

For example, if you purchased a used car in cash for $2,500 it may not be worth it to purchase a full coverage insurance policy. The cost of the full coverage policy will likely amount to more than what the vehicle is worth over a short period of time.

Ask your insurance company to provide you with a quote for each deductible that is available. A deductible is the amount of money that you will have to pay in order to file an insurance claim after an accident or claimable incident occurs. Higher deductibles equate to lower insurance premiums, and the inverse relationship occurs in that lower deductibles will result in a higher premium.

The standard deductibles offered are usually $250 or $500. I recommend staying away from significantly low or high deductibles such as $100 or $1,000, because of the amount of money that a low deductible will usually increase your annual premium, and because paying $1,000 when an accident or unexpected event occurs could result in significant financial struggles.

Take careful notes for each vehicle that you are looking at, and ensure that you consider this information when deciding on the car that you are going to purchase. Researching the cost of insurance prior to purchasing a car is an important step because it will prevent you from being blindsided by high insurance premiums, and will ensure that you are not wasting your time looking at cars that you can't afford to properly insure.

The last step that you need to take before going to look at and test drive the vehicles that you have included on your list (if you are applying for a loan) is to call your bank and see what financing you qualify for. The loan amount that your bank will approve for you is highly dependent on factors such as your credit score, credit history, income, current amount of debt, length of the loan, and if you are purchasing a new or a used vehicle. When calling your bank, simply request to be pre-approved for an auto loan and supply the appropriate information that the lender requests.

It is not always advantageous to take a loan from your personal bank while purchasing a vehicle. Sometimes, car dealerships will have special financing promotions that you may qualify for, or they are able to offer a financing deal on new vehicles with an interest rate that is lower than what your bank offered.

However, there are a couple of reasons why you need to call your bank prior to going to the dealership. First, this will give you a general idea on if you are going to be able to secure financing for the vehicle that you are looking at. There is no point of test driving a vehicle with a $20,000 price tag if you are only able to secure financing for $12,000; proper research will ensure that you don't waste your time and will help you set realistic expectations for yourself. Second, this will allow you to know if the interest rate that a dealership offers you is fair or not.

It is important for you to realize that car dealerships make huge profits every year by securing loans at higher interest rates than what you actually qualified for.

How do dealerships make money off of your loan? When the dealership offers you a loan, and tells you that you are approved for $10,000 at a 7% interest rate for a term of 60 months, that dealership is not actually the one giving you the loan; it is simply finding a loan for you through one of their preferred lenders. The bank will supply the dealership with a loan option, and then the dealership adds on what is known as a "finance reserve" to the interest rate before telling you what the terms of the loan that you are approved for are. That's right, you may have been approved for a 5% interest rate, and the sales manager at the dealership simply tells you that you were approved for a loan with an 8% interest rate, and profits off of the difference.

In most cases, the finance reserve that the dealership will add on is between one and three percent, but this could vary and be substantially higher if the dealership that you are shopping at thinks that they can make a higher profit from securing your loan. A good way to think of the finance reserve is to view it as the dealership's commission for finding you a loan.

Understand that you can negotiate the finance reserve, and that merely bringing this up to the sales manager of the dealership will send a signal that shows you are somewhat competent in the car buying process. If the interest rate that the dealership offers you is substantially higher than the rate your bank offered you, it is likely because of the finance reserve that the dealership is attempting to place on your loan.

After speaking with your bank and gaining some perspective on the financing options that are available to you, it is finally time to go and test drive the vehicles on your list. Since you did your research, you should be able to go to a dealership that has the vehicle you are looking for available for sale.

Never purchase a vehicle that you have not driven, and ensure that you drive it for at least thirty minutes during the test drive. Don't feel rushed by the salesperson during the test drive, and take the vehicle to locations where you can experience different driving conditions; remember that you are the customer, and should be treated as such. Test driving the vehicle on the highway, through a few neighborhoods, in high-traffic areas, and through some shopping complexes will give you an idea for how the vehicle is going to handle and perform in different environments. This will allow you to see if the vehicle has blind spots that make it hard for you to see, how the brakes work, what happens when the vehicle heats up, and how the car handles while going over speed bumps or in the everyday situations that you normally drive in.

After the test drive is complete, ensure that you perform a thorough inspection of the inside and outside of the vehicle. Check for any type of damage that could suggest the vehicle has been in an accident, as well as small scratches, rust, corrosion, and for things that could be missing such as the spare tire or jack.

If the vehicle is used, ensure to ask the salesperson if the car has ever been in an accident before. Regardless of the answer they provide, request that a Carfax report is pulled on the vehicle and shown to you. This report will show if any major repairs have been made on the vehicle due to a collision. Unless your financial situation keeps you from doing so, try to stay away from vehicles that have collisions listed on the Carfax report. The body shop may have done a great job when repairing the vehicle, but this will always have a negative impact on the vehicle's resale value when you decide to sell or trade the car in on a later date.

Consider the condition that the vehicle is in, and compare it to what your research shows that the vehicle is worth; then come up with a price that the data and your research shows the vehicle is worth.

If you like the vehicle and feel that it meets all of your needs, then it is time to talk to the salesperson about the price, and to start the negotiation step of the car buying process. There are a few dealerships, such as CarMax, that simply do not ever negotiate their price, but most dealerships expect to negotiate and they will factor a slight increase into the price to compensate for it.

Most likely, the price that is listed on the vehicle's sticker is higher than the price that you had in mind after conducting your research. When you sit down with your salesperson, you have to make your case for the price that you want to pay, and stick to it. Simply throwing out a number that is 5% lower than the sticker price, without being able to justify your reasoning isn't going to work well with most sales managers. You want to get a good deal, but you also have to be realistic and fair in your offer; the only way to ensure that you do this is through proper research.

This is the time when you need to explain why the price you have in mind is fair for all parties involved, and that you are not going to purchase a vehicle for more than it is truly worth. Use the research you have conducted, and justify the price that you tell the salesperson you will purchase the vehicle for.

In most instances, the salesperson will have to talk to the sales manager, and will come back to the table with an amount that is higher than what you said you are willing to purchase the vehicle for. This is when you have to stick to your price and be confident in the research that you conducted. Tell the salesperson that the vehicle is simply not worth the amount of money that they are asking you to pay for it, justify your response with your research, and restate that you will not be purchasing the vehicle for a price that is any higher than the one you mentioned.

Recognize the fact that you may be tempted to purchase the vehicle for slightly higher than your original number because the dealership came down on their price, or because you feel that it is close enough to the price that you had in mind, don't do it. Don't allow yourself to purchase a vehicle for a price that is higher than what your research has determined it is worth!  Doing this is the same as giving someone six one dollar bills, when they ask if you can break a five; it simply doesn't make any financial sense.

The negotiation process should end in one of two ways; either you purchase the vehicle for the price that your research determined is fair, or you walk out of the dealership and start the process over again with another vehicle or another dealership. Although walking out can feel like a loss at the time, realize that you made a good financial decision because you did not overpay for a vehicle.

Also, walking out of the dealership can be used as a negotiation tactic.  If you don't feel as if you are getting anywhere in regards to lowering the price, tell your salesperson that you are leaving, and leave them your contact information in case they decide that they would like to sell the vehicle for the amount that you offered them.  There have been many instances where this strategy has resulted in a phone call from the sales manger within fifteen minutes after leaving the dealership, stating that they would like for you to come back to purchase the vehicle at the price you offered.

Something to realize about the negotiation process is that it is not a "one size fits all" strategy. People who have different personalities, experiences, and those who are in different financial situations may have different strategies that they feel more comfortable with.  However, the one thing that remains consistent throughout the negotiation process is the importance of research.  It is through your research that you can feel confident throughout the negotiation process and stick to your price. This research will also provide you with the confidence that you made the correct decision if you have to walk away from a vehicle that you really liked, because the numbers simply did not line up.

Additionally, it is important to remember that the dealership has to make a little bit of money. Although we want to get the best deal possible, you cannot throw an unreasonable offer on the table that is not based on any data, and expect the sales manager to lose money for their dealership. Conduct your research, and then offer a price that is fair and can be justified.

Hopefully, the salesperson and you will be able to agree on the fair price that you offered. After you agree to the price and say that you would like to purchase the vehicle, the rest of the transaction will likely take place in the finance office. While in the finance office, you will discuss the way that you are going to pay for the vehicle (with either a loan or cash), and may be offered items such as gap insurance and an extended warranty. Most dealerships make over 30% of their annual profits from the finance reserve, and selling insurance or warranties, so realize what you are walking into!

Since have you conducted research and called your bank to get pre-approved for a loan prior to stepping into the dealership, you will know right away if the loan that the dealership found for you is reasonable or not. Remember that the dealership will have a finance reserve attached to the interest rate they are offering you.

Ask the person in the finance office how much of a finance reserve is being placed on the loan that they are offering you? The terms or language that they may use to identify the finance reserve is the difference between the "buy rate" and the "sell rate".

Understand that the dealership is not going to want to show you this information. In fact, they may even act like they are appalled that you asked! However, don't be discouraged from asking to see this information or to know what it is; in the end, this is your money that you are spending and you should know where it is going.

Most likely, the dealership is going to put a higher finance reserve on the first loan that they offer you; this is to see your reaction, and to see if you will bite on a loan that results in a higher commission for them.

You need to be on guard while in the finance office, and realize how much money an extra percent or two will cost you over the long-run. For instance, the difference between a 5% interest rate and a 7% interest rate on a five year loan for $25,000 will result in you paying an additional $1,395 over the lifetime of the loan. With that example, it is easy to see how dealerships make their money through financing. The real kicker is that dealerships will sometimes obtain finance reserves in the amount of seven to ten percent; this occurs because most people do not conduct diligent research, and are unaware of the fact that the dealership is adding a commission for themselves to their loan.

Most of the time, refusing the first loan that is offered to you, talking about the finance reserve (or buy and sell rate), and informing the finance person at the dealership that you will only finance through them if they can beat the rate offered by your bank, will result in the dealership trying to find the best deal for you so that they can sell a vehicle. If the dealership cannot beat your bank's rate, then simply call your bank and tell them that you would like to go forward with the loan that you have been pre-approved for.

Next, let's cover gap insurance! Gap insurance is simply an insurance policy that covers the difference of what you owe on a vehicle, and what it is worth, in the case of a collision or if your vehicle is stolen. For instance, if your vehicle is only worth $10,000 but you owe $14,000 and are involved in a collision that results in your vehicle being totaled, gap insurance will pay the $4,000 difference to your lender so that you don't have to. Without gap insurance, your insurance company will only pay up to what the vehicle's current value is, and you are left on the hook to pay off the remainder of your loan. If you do not have the additional funds required to pay off the loan, you will be stuck paying a car payment for a car that you cannot drive or no longer have.

Is gap insurance a good idea and should you purchase it from the dealership? The decision to purchase gap insurance or not depends on if you are purchasing a new or used vehicle, if you are putting a down payment on the vehicle, and your overall financial situation. Understand that a new vehicle becomes a used vehicle the moment that you pull out of the dealership parking lot, which results in a significant loss of value.  Most new vehicles will lose about 30% of their value within the first year, and an additional 15-20% in the year after that.  This causes your vehicle to be worth substantially less than what you owe on it, and this will be the case until you make the first few years of payments.

If you know that you are going to owe a significant amount more than what the vehicle is worth, and that you are not in the financial situation to cover the amount that would remain on your loan in the case of a collision or theft, then you should entertain the idea of getting gap insurance.

However, you do not have to purchase gap insurance from the dealership!  Once again, do not buy gap insurance from a car dealership!  Most car dealerships will make you feel like gap insurance is a once in a lifetime opportunity, and that you will forever regret not purchasing the policy from them; this is not true!  There are numerous insurance companies that offer gap insurance, and the policy will be significantly cheaper than what you will be able to purchase it for at a dealership.  Most likely, your insurance company will provide you with the best deal on gap insurance, but it is still important that you call around and get quotes from a few other sources.

Also note that you are able to receive a refund on your gap insurance policy if you trade in, pay off, or sell your vehicle before the term of the loan is up. When you purchase a gap insurance policy, it covers the full term of the loan. If you sell your vehicle early, you can call the insurance company and receive a pro-rated refund; this refund will be for a percentage of the original policy, and in accordance with how much time was remaining on the loan when it was paid off. Some insurance companies have different terms or regulations when it comes to refunds, so make sure to ask while shopping for the policy.

The next item that is sure to come up in the finance office is an extended warranty. It is important to realize that the prices of these warranties are very negotiable. This is an item that dealerships make a substantial commission from, and the salesperson is willing to take a small cut in their commission rather than make nothing at all. Some of the warranty plans that are offered in a dealership are able to be negotiated down 40-50 percent!

The employees that work in the finance department are usually rated on their ability to sell extended warranties as well. This means that when it is time for the employee's review or to be judged on their performance, their ability to sell extended warranties is going to be factored into how good they are at their job.

As a negotiation technique, it is always a good idea to turn down the extended warranty right away; while doing this, mention that the price is simply way too high and that you won't pay that amount for a warranty. Most of the time, the response from the salesperson will be a drastic cut in the price of the warranty.

The decision to purchase a warranty is going to be different for each person and each type of vehicle. Some vehicles have great factory warranties that will last for the entire time that you are planning to own the vehicle. If you only drive ten thousand miles per year, and are purchasing a new vehicle with a five year loan, it is likely that your vehicle will be covered by the factory warranty until the vehicle is paid off.

However, if you drive a lot and are planning to keep the vehicle well past the time that the factory warranty is going to last, you need to analyze your finances and determine how you are going to handle something such as your transmission going out, or serious engine problems. You may find that it is worth it to pay slightly more money per month, in order to have the peace of mind associated with knowing that you will not have to pay for unexpected and costly repairs in the future.

If you decide to purchase an extended warranty, ensure that you look closely at the different packages that are offered. Most of the time, dealerships will have standard, silver, gold, or platinum packages that you can choose from. Usually, the standard package that covers the power train for an extended period of years and mileage amount is all that you need. Other packages that include rental vehicles, towing, and free oil changes will likely end up costing you more in the end; this is especially true if you are including the price of the extended warranty into your loan, and paying interest on the additional cost for the next five years.

Lastly, make sure to ask about the deductible and any stipulations that are associated with the extended warranty that you are purchasing. It is important to know what dealerships or repair facilities are permitted to work on the vehicle, and what the deductible will be if you have to take your vehicle in for a repair. Some extended warranty plans will require you to take your vehicle to a specific dealership or repair facility, while others will allow you to take the vehicle to any certified repair shop.

While signing all of the paperwork at the dealership for the loan or warranty, ensure to get anything that was promised to you throughout the entire transaction in writing. For instance, if the floor mats were missing and your salesperson said they will get you new ones, make sure that a "we owe" is signed and that you receive a copy. A "we owe" is simply a form signed by the dealership that outlines any promises or items that the buyer is owed in the future. Without this form, the dealership is not on the hook for anything that they said or promised you during the transaction.

Now that we have extensively covered the process of purchasing a vehicle at a dealership and how to watch out for some of the tricks that are out there, let's go over some things to be aware of when purchasing a car over the internet or from a private seller. First, you must realize that there are a lot of con-artists and dishonest people who will try to take advantage of you on the various "for sale by owner" websites. Be cautious of everyone that you meet or talk to, and be sure to ask a lot of questions about the car, why they are selling it, and previous mechanical problems. If the purchase seems like it is too good to be true, it probably is. Follow your gut when dealing with anyone online; if you have a bad feeling about the deal or person, walk away immediately.

If you decide that you want to look at a vehicle that you found online, only agree to meet the seller in a public setting, and bring someone else with you for added safety. Inform the seller that you will need to see their driver's license, vehicle registration, and proof of insurance prior to test driving the car. If any of this is a problem, do not waste your time going to look at the car because it is likely a scam. Also request that the seller brings the title for the vehicle so that you can ensure the VIN number on the car matches what the title says. The last thing that you want to do is purchase a stolen car!

If everything with the car's seller goes well and you liked the vehicle when you test drove it, the next thing to do is to take the vehicle to an automotive shop to have an inspection completed. Most of the time, you can get a certified mechanic to conduct a thorough inspection on a vehicle for around $75; this could end up saving you hundreds or thousands of dollars in the long run if it prevents you from purchasing a car that is showing signs of a major problem. Remember, sometimes people will try to get rid of their vehicle because something is starting to go wrong with it, and they want to dump it before it is too late.

After the inspection has been completed, if you decide that you would like to purchase the vehicle, make sure to complete the proper documentation. Completing the paperwork that your state requires will ensure that you have a record of the purchase, but it will also make it easier for you to get insurance and register your new vehicle.

A document that you and the seller need to sign is a "bill of sale". This document does not have to be in a specific format or include a bunch of legal terms in order to be valid. The purpose of the bill of sale is to simply outline what is being sold/purchased, who the people selling and buying the vehicle are, the price of the sale, and any stipulations regarding the sale. Ensure to list the year, make, model, and VIN number of the vehicle, and then both parties need to sign the document in the presence of a notary public.

Next, I recommend going to the bank with the seller and completing the rest of the transaction there. This is a great place to finish the transaction because you will have access to your funds, but also because if there was ever a chance that you are dealing with a scam artist, the last place they will want to go is a bank that has hundreds of cameras recording them. Get a cashier's check from your bank in the amount that is due, and only hand it over after the seller signs the vehicle's title over to you.

I cannot stress this one point enough to you; if at any time your gut is telling you that something is not right or off about the person selling you their vehicle, walk away immediately. There are people who prey on inexperienced, elderly, or naïve car buyers all over the internet who can be very convincing, trust your gut!

The last area that we need to cover in regards to buying a vehicle is the decision to lease a car. Leasing a vehicle simply means that when you are done making your payments for the agreed upon term, you will give the vehicle back to the dealership instead of owning it. A lease is originated by providing the dealership with a down payment and signing agreed upon terms. This option is attractive to some drivers because they can get a new or more reliable vehicle for a lower monthly payment than they could if they tried to purchase it.

If you are considering leasing a vehicle instead of purchasing one, there are a few things that you need to consider and be aware of throughout the process. First, you need to go back to the self-evaluation step that we covered earlier in this chapter and look at how many miles that you drive per year. All leases will have a yearly mileage outlined in the agreement. For instance, if you sign a four year lease with a 12,000 mile per year limit, you will have to pay an additional charge for every mile that you drove over 48,000 miles during the term of the lease. Every lease agreement is different in regards to how much the fee per mile will cost, but it tends to average between twelve and thirty cents per mile.

Most leases come standard with a mileage limit between 12,000 and 15,000 miles. If you commute a longer distance or there is a possibility that you are going to put more miles per year on the vehicle than that, you can pay a higher monthly payment to receive a higher mileage limit. The important take away from this, is that you never want to put yourself in a position where going over the mileage limit outlined in the lease's terms is a possibility.

Almost all leases are going to require some form of down payment. Although putting a higher down payment on the lease will lower your monthly payment, it is important to understand that if the vehicle is stolen or in a collision that results in the vehicle being totaled, your insurance company is still only going to pay the amount that the vehicle is worth after depreciation, which could lead to your down payment being wasted.

Higher down payments are wasted when the person leasing the vehicle has gap insurance and an incident occurs early on in the terms of the lease. The same analysis that was considered in regards to gap insurance for purchasing a vehicle needs to be considered while leasing a vehicle. Understand that if you have gap insurance and the vehicle is totaled in a collision or stolen, the gap insurance will only pay the difference of what is owed and the value of the vehicle; if you placed a large down payment on the leased vehicle and had to make an insurance claim, you would essentially be losing the money you gave as a down payment.

Another factor to consider when leasing a vehicle is the length of the lease. Most leases are for a period of two to four years. It is important to look at the length of the "bumper to bumper" warranty that comes with the vehicle that you are leasing and ensure that the length of the lease does not extend past that warranty. The last thing that you want to do is have to make costly repairs to a vehicle that you know you are not going to own in the near future.

When the lease term has been completed, the dealership that you have to return the vehicle to is going to conduct a damage and vehicle condition assessment. This assessment will determine if there is excessive damage to the vehicle, or if the vehicle has simply undergone normal wear and tear. Prior to signing a lease, ensure that you look at the "lease-end conditions" so that you are aware of what is considered normal wear and tear, and what is considered damage that you will have to pay for.

Lastly, when your lease term comes to an end you will likely be given the option to purchase the vehicle that you leased. This is referred to as "buying out" your lease. Dealerships have to spend time and money to transport, clean, and sell a vehicle after a lease expires; therefore, they would much rather sell a leased vehicle directly to the leasee, instead of going through the hassle and added expenses associated with selling the vehicle to someone else. If the car still meets your needs and you decide that you want to keep it, you may be able to get a good deal through buying out your lease.

A lease can also be bought out early. For instance, if a four year lease has been signed but you decide that you would like to purchase the car after two years, you can negotiate a price with the leasing company, and purchase the vehicle before the term of the lease expires. Understand that you will likely have to pay an early termination fee for buying out a lease before the original terms expire.

Buying out a lease early can be a great option to avoid paying for damage that is not considered normal wear and tear, or excessive mileage fees. If you lease a vehicle and end up in a situation where you know that you are going to go over the mileage limitations, it may be a better option for you to buy out your lease early, than to hold onto it and pay the additional fees in the end.

It is important that you take all of the topics covered in this chapter into consideration while embarking on the adventure of purchasing or leasing a vehicle. Remember the importance of research and how necessary it is in order to negotiate properly, while also being on guard for dealerships that try to make excessive profits from insurance policies or your financing offer. Conduct ample research, stick to your price, be on guard of scams, and use the information you have to get the car that you need and can afford.

# FIVE

## INVESTING BASICS

Saving for retirement is one of the most
important things that you will ever have to do in your
life; yet there is not a class that teaches the most basic
functions of investing at a majority of high schools.
This is an area where most education systems are
severely failing students and young adults.

A majority of high school graduates are
unaware of the differences between a Roth and
Traditional IRA, how the stock market works, what
the S&P 500 is, the benefits of a mutual fund, or

where to begin when trying to invest for their future. This is a problem that needs to be confronted immediately, because it is resulting in a large percentage of our Nation's young adults to miss out on the most beneficial investing years of their lifetime.

Senior citizens and individuals currently over the age of 60, say that the largest mistake they made during their lifetime, in regards to finances, was that they did not start saving for retirement early enough, or at all. Surveys taken in the year of 2017 showed that less than 15% of people who are over the age of 60 have enough money in a retirement account to sustain themselves without having to work after their 67th birthday. Bottom line: If you want to enjoy your retirement years, the best step that you can take now is to start investing a set amount of money each month into a retirement account, and increase it as you are able to.

As an example, and using the average growth rate of the entire stock market over the past 100 years, a person who invested just $100 per month for 30 years would end up with over $186,000 at the end of the 30 year period. Surely, this is not enough money to retire, but keep in mind that this amount of money is based on only investing $100 per month or a total of $36,000 over the 30 year period. Think back to the chapter on budgeting and remember that it is recommended to allocate at least 10% of your income towards some type of savings or retirement account each month.

It is important that you don't allow yourself to make excuses for why you are not saving for retirement. The payment that you are making to yourself needs to be non-negotiable, and an item included in your budget that is never discounted or disregarded. Think of it as a bill from a creditor, and letting it go unpaid for even one month it is not an option!

Putting money in a standard savings account at your bank each month is not a beneficial way to save for retirement; you simply will not be able to accrue a large enough nest egg with the low interest rates that savings accounts provide to build a sufficient savings for retirement. To understand the reason why a standard savings account is not enough to save for retirement, you first need to know what inflation is and how it adversely affects the value of a dollar over time. In simple terms, **inflation** refers to the increase in prices throughout the economy as a whole, or how the value of a dollar shrinks over time by a certain percentage.

For example, when your grandmother told you the story about how she was able to purchase a gumball with a penny as a child, and now it costs a quarter, this is due to inflation. The **time value of money** refers to the idea that a dollar bill which you have in your possession right now, will always be worth less in the future. If the inflation percentage for this year is 2%, the same dollar bill that you are holding in your hand right now will only be worth $0.98 next year; this is because the prices of all available products in the marketplace have increased by 2% throughout the year. The historic average of annual inflation rates for the United States is slightly over 3.2%, which equates to the prices of products and services nearly doubling every twenty years, due to compounding inflation.

The average savings account only pays an interest rate of about one tenth of one percent per year. It becomes very apparent when you do a little bit of simple math that it doesn't make financial sense to have your retirement savings in an account that only makes one tenth of one percent in interest, while inflation is averaging over 3.2%; you are actually losing money when you keep money in a savings account for long periods of time. This is why understanding how the stock market works is critical to building a sustainable retirement account that will grow at a higher rate than inflation. You simply cannot save for retirement successfully without incorporating items available to you in the stock market.

Throughout this chapter, the significance of starting to invest for your retirement early will become very apparent. Basic terms such as stocks, bonds, Roth IRA's, mutual funds, the NASDAQ, dividends, and a few others are going to be covered in depth, and at a level that is easy for a new investor to understand. We are going to go through the steps of setting up a retirement account, talk about levels of risk, and ensure that you have all of the information that you need in order to confidently start a basic retirement account that will best position you for the future.

Understand that the focus of this chapter will be on saving for retirement and the basics of investing; this is not a chapter on how to get rich quick, or on making speculative investments. In no way am I advising you on how to invest, what to invest in, or guaranteeing that you are going to make a profit. I encourage you to read about different investing strategies, and to educate yourself about the ins and outs of the stock market, but caution you against taking too much stake or getting caught up in a "get rich quick" scheme or investment strategy. Retirement investing is done slowly, carefully, consistently, and by appropriately managing risk in accordance with your age, income, and retirement goals; there are no tricks or short-cuts.

The stock market is an ever changing, huge, complex, and confusing beast. For people who have never been taught the ins and outs of the market, investing towards retirement is sure to be a daunting, frightening, and challenging task. To begin, we are going to start by explaining some of the basic and fundamental terms that are associated with investing and the stock market.

So what is a **stock** and why do corporations sell *shares* of stock? A good way to define a share of stock is to think of it as a small portion of a company. Although this definition isn't 100% accurate because you don't actually own the assets associated with the company that you purchase stock in, this definition will keep you in the right mindset when it comes to basic investing.

The real difference between being an owner of a company and owning shares of stock, is that owners can make decisions regarding a company's assets, business operations, and products, while shareholders of stock simply benefit from the profits that a corporation makes, and will not typically have the right to make decisions associated with the company's operations, products, or services. For instance, buying a few shares of stock in a technology company does not give you the right to make decisions pertaining to the new line of phones, computers, watches, or tablets being developed. However, if the company's profits and the stock price increases, you will likely receive a percentage of that profit in accordance to the amount of shares that you own.

Corporations issue shares of stock, or sell part of the company to investors, in order to fund expansion efforts and to pay for business operations. As investors purchase shares of stock, that money is used by the company to pay employees, purchase equipment, buy buildings needed for expansion, pay for advertising, and anything else that needs to be funded in order for the company to deliver its product or service to customers. This is how corporate America works, and how large companies are able to fund extensive projects.

Investors make money from purchasing stocks in one of two ways, through an increase in the stock's price, or by receiving dividends. Making a profit from an increase in the stock's price is pretty simple to understand; if you purchase a share of stock for

$40, and it goes up to $50, you made a profit of $10. A **dividend** is an established percentage that a company agrees to pay to its shareholders, usually paid quarterly. For instance, if a company has a quarterly dividend of 0.25%, shareholders will receive that amount when the company pays out its quarterly dividend, in accordance to the amount of shares that they own.

Dividends are a way that corporations reward shareholders for holding stock, and to return profits to investors. Some companies decide to pay dividends; others decide to hold profits inside of the company for future investment opportunities. Corporations that are known for paying out a substantial dividend every quarter are usually referred to as "income stocks", while corporations that do not pay dividends are labeled as "growth stocks".

Another way that a corporation raises money to fund its operations is through selling bonds. A **bond** is essentially a loan that a company is taking from an investor (you). As the investor, you are similar to the bank when compared to normal loans that you may be familiar with. In simple terms, when a company sells a bond, it is taking a loan from the investor for a specific period of time, with the promise to pay back the loan's full amount at the end of the designated time period, and a specified interest rate along the way is paid to the investor. In other words, if you invest $1,000 in a bond, you will accumulate interest throughout the period that you hold the bond, and then will also receive your original $1,000 investment back when the bond expires. Interest paid to the bondholder is often referred to as the **coupon** rate.

The rate of interest, or coupon rate, associated with different bonds will vary depending upon how risky the bond is, and how many years the bond is good for. Companies that are struggling financially may pay a higher coupon rate on its bonds because the company is more desperate for money, and the investment carries more risk for the investor; this also means that the risk of the company claiming bankruptcy or not being able to pay back bondholders is higher.

The term **junk bond** may be used to describe bonds with larger coupon rates or higher risk. Junk bonds are non-investment grade bonds and have a lower rating by the agencies responsible for evaluating the amount of risk associated with a bond.

The longer the term of the bond, the higher the interest rate tends to be; this is because companies need to offer a higher interest rate to keep your money for a longer period of time. The safest bond that you can purchase as an investor is a treasury bond; this also means that treasury bonds can have some of the lowest coupon rates, because you are not taking on as much risk. These are bonds that you are purchasing from the United States Treasury, and they carry the lowest amount of risk because the United States has never defaulted on its bonds.

As a young investor (twenties or thirties), treasury bonds should not amount to a large percentage of assets in your retirement portfolio; this is because you have a much higher risk-tolerance, which we will get into a little later in this chapter, and can choose other investment instruments that are likely to provide you with a higher return at an acceptable level of risk.

Another thing to keep in mind when investing in bonds is that sometimes corporations reserve the right to "call back" bonds earlier than the date originally outlined. These bonds are referred to as **callable bonds** and corporations may use their option to call back a bond earlier than expected if changes in the market or interest rates favor doing so.

Understand that a corporation will continuously evaluate its ability to secure financing at a lower cost, while considering all associated risks and market factors. After all, the number one responsibility of a corporation's management board is to make the largest profit possible for its shareholders. In simpler terms, a company that calls back a bond will "pay off" the bondholder earlier than expected, so that they do not have to continue paying the investor interest throughout the bond's original expiration date when it is not financially advantageous to do so.

Now let's move onto the markets. If you ever watch the news or look at a website that gives information pertaining to the stock market, you are sure to hear terms such as the "Dow", "S&P 500", or "NASDAQ". These names or labels are associated with averages, indices, or groups of large corporations that have been identified to represent the stock market, or a group of stocks, as a whole.

The Dow is one of the most watched stock indices (technically averages) throughout the world, and is composed of 30 highly reputable and well-known corporations; these corporations are believed by some to best represent the entire economy. Some of the corporations that are included in the Dow are McDonalds, 3M, Exxon Mobile, Johnson and Johnson, Nike, and IBM.

This average was originally developed by Charles Dow and Edward Jones in 1896 with only 12 corporations included, but was changed to include 30 corporations in 1928. The Dow is the oldest of all stock averages, and is calculated as a "price-weighted index"; this simply means that the corporations with the highest share price carry the most weight in the Dow Jones Industrial Average. When the market closes, the Dow is calculated by adding the share prices of the 30 corporations together, and dividing by what is known as the Dow Jones Industrial Average Divisor. This divisor originally started as the number of stocks included in the average, but due to events such as stock "splits" and the addition of new corporations into the Dow, a complex divisor has been created.

Overall, the Dow is simply a list of 30 corporations that are believed by some to best represent all areas of the U.S. economy; therefore it includes the stock of some of the largest and most well-known corporations form a range of sectors such as banking, energy, technology, healthcare, and transportation.

The next well-known index is the Standard and Poor's 500, often referred to as the S&P 500. Stocks in the S&P 500 are ranked based on the company's market capitalization (its overall value), instead of the price of the stock. Guidelines are established by economists at Standard and Poor's to determine which companies are permitted to be a part of the S&P 500. Corporations need to have a market capitalization of at least $6.1 billion, and meet scrupulous reporting standards to ensure transparency in all financial records before being listed in the S&P 500.

The name S&P 500 is present because there are 500 corporations that make up this index. As the value of each company changes throughout the trading day, so does the S&P 500. This index has become a highly preferred tool for investors because of the large amount of companies and different sectors of the economy that are represented.

The last index that you may be familiar with is the NASDAQ (National Association of Securities Dealers Automated Quotations). Similar to the Dow and S&P 500, this is a group of corporations that have been put together to represent the market, or a part of the market. The differentiating factor of the NASDAQ is that this index primarily focuses on technology companies. It is calculated in accordance with a company's market capitalization (overall value), just like the S&P 500.

Overall, the Dow, S&P 500, and NASDAQ are simply a way for investors to obtain a snap-shot of how the stock market, or a sector of the market, is performing. These indices will become very important later on in this chapter when we discuss setting up a retirement account that is diversified. An account that is **diversified** means that the account is composed of a wide-array of companies or investments; in other words, you are not investing everything you have in one company. I encourage you to search some financial websites and to take a look at the Dow, S&P 500, and NASDAQ. Try to dive into which companies make up each group, and look at how each index has changed over the past few years or decades by evaluating graphs that depict different lengths of time.

The next term, and very important investing instrument that you will hear frequently when speaking about investing is a **mutual fund**. A mutual fund is managed by a professional fund manager, and is simply a pool of money that is collected from numerous investors in order to purchase a group of stocks, bonds, or other investment instruments. Mutual funds are highly beneficial in retirement saving because they allow investors to purchase a wide array of stocks, bonds, or other investing instruments, without having to purchase a share of stock or a bond in each corporation. Understanding the benefits of purchasing mutual funds for your retirement account is one of the most important parts of this chapter, so listen up!

Here is an example of how a mutual fund works: Let's say that John would like to invest in all of the companies listed in the S&P 500 at one time, but can only afford to invest a total of $500. It is not possible for John to purchase a share of stock in each company, because the total cost associated with purchasing shares in each company far exceeds the $500 that John is willing to invest. Instead, John purchases a mutual fund that matches the S&P 500; therefore, when the S&P 500 increases three percent, so does John's mutual fund. Mutual funds are available with a variety of price points, meaning that you can purchase a share in a mutual fund that matches the S&P 500 for $5, $10, or $100, depending on which mutual fund you choose to invest in.

How is this possible? The financial institution or bank that John is investing through simply pools together a group of investors' money to make the larger purchase. There are mutual funds that incorporate large groups of international stocks, smaller companies, bonds, technology sectors, and the list is almost endless. This is how an investor, who does not have a large amount of money to start with, is able to create a diversified retirement or investment account, also known as a portfolio.

Before diving into how we can use stocks, bonds, and mutual funds to save for retirement, let's take a break and dive into setting up a retirement account, such as an IRA (Individual Retirement Account) so that you can gain an understanding of what you are purchasing these investment instruments for, and so that you understand how to create an account to put your stocks, bonds, or mutual funds in once you purchase them.

Before purchasing stocks, bonds, or mutual funds, you need to set up an account to put these investments in. When saving for retirement, the account that you are going to set up is an Individual Retirement Account (IRA). When trying to understand what an IRA is, it is easy to think of it as the box that you are going to put all of your investments inside of.

The benefits of setting up an IRA instead of just purchasing investments and letting them sit in a brokerage account, is the tax benefits that you will receive over time. If you choose the wrong type of account, you could end up forfeiting large portions of your profit through paying taxes at an undesirable time. The two types of IRAs available to you are "Roth" and "Traditional" IRAs, and the most differentiating factors are when you are taxed, and penalties associated with withdrawing funds before the age of 59 ½.

The amount of money that you are allowed to contribute to an IRA is $5,500 per year until you are the age of 50, and then the amount increases to $6,500 per year in order to allow for older investors to catch up or invest more before they retire.

In a Roth IRA, the income that you contribute (through the purchase of stocks, bonds, mutual funds, etc.) is taxed at the time you put money into the account. You are not able to deduct this contribution from your income as an expense during your yearly tax filing, but this means that you will not be taxed on it when withdrawing it during your retirement years (or if you decide to pull it out earlier).

Taxes for a Traditional IRA are handled exactly opposite, whereas the contributions made throughout the year are able to be deducted from your income when filing your annual tax return, but you will pay taxes when withdrawing funds during your retirement years.

So which is better: Roth or Traditional? This depends on how much money you currently make, and how much you think that you are going to make during your retirement years. The tax code is currently set up using an income bracket system; in other words, the more money that you make, the more you are taxed. The goal here is to pay as little amount of tax as possible on your money!

If you are in a low-income tax bracket, currently making less money now or during your working years than you think you will once you retire, it is more beneficial for you to set up a Roth IRA. This is because your annual contributions will be taxed at the lower tax rate, rather than at the higher tax rate that you will fall into once you retire.

On the other hand, if you are currently in a high paying career, making more money per year than you will likely receive during your retirement years, it is more beneficial for you to set up a Traditional IRA. This way, you will be able to deduct the amount that you contribute to your retirement fund each year when completing your annual tax return, and pay a lower tax rate when you withdrawal the money during your retirement years.

Let's use John and Sue as examples to gain a better understanding of how each type of IRA works.

John currently makes $50,000 per year and is a diligent investor. He saves a minimum of 10% of his income and follows a disciplined plan to invest for retirement. Because of John's annual salary, he has a little bit of debt such as a car payment, and will likely have to pay a mortgage payment during some of his retirement years. With his investment strategy and income during retirement, John plans on being able to receive $100,000 per year once he retires. In this scenario, the better choice for John would be to set up a Roth IRA, because he will be taxed in accordance with making $50,000 per year instead of waiting until retirement and being taxed on his income of $100,000 per year.

On the other hand, Sue is a doctor currently making $200,000 per year. Like John, she is a diligent investor and is saving for retirement. Because of her high income, Sue is able to pay off her house at a fairly young age, has no debt, and very little bills. When Sue retires, she only plans on needing $100,000 per year to live on (half of her current income). The better choice for Sue would be to choose a Traditional IRA; this is because she will be taxed during the time she is making $100,000 per year, rather than being taxed when she is in her working years and making $200,000 per year.

The last important differentiating factor between a Roth and Traditional IRA is the investor's ability to withdrawal funds. In a Roth IRA, there is not a penalty for withdrawing money that you contributed (this does not include money that you earned through interest or gains) before the age of

59½.  This is because all of the money that has been contributed to a Roth IRA has already been taxed, and belongs to you.  On the other hand, withdrawing from a Traditional IRA will cost you an additional 10% tax penalty.  Of course, the goal of saving for retirement is not to touch the money, but it is understood that life or death emergencies occur and priorities can change.

To set up the IRA that you decide is appropriate for your circumstances, you can choose to go through a large named bank that offers investment services (most well known banks offer this), or an investment company such as Vanguard, Fidelity, TD Ameritrade, E-Trade, or the numerous other companies that offer investment services.  A quick online search with "set up an IRA" will provide you with a variety of options.  If you prefer to have someone that you can speak with in person, a large bank may best fit your needs; however, online options have become increasingly popular because of lower fees, easy accessibility, and the wide array of funds available to investors.

Let's read through an example (and my recommendation for how new investors should get started) of how you can start investing towards your retirement right now, with the basic knowledge that you have learned throughout this chapter.

EXAMPLE:  In the year of 2017, John is 20 years old, plans to retire around the year of 2060, and wants to set up a Roth IRA to start saving for retirement.  After completing some research online, John chooses to set up a Roth IRA with Vanguard.

Although John is a novice investor, he knows that he wants his portfolio to be diversified, and at an appropriate risk level for his age.

John looks through the mutual funds that Vanguard offers and finds one labeled "Vanguard Target Retirement 2060 Fund". This fund is managed by a Vanguard Fund Manager, and contains the appropriate ratio of stocks and bonds that someone retiring in 2060 would want. John decides to purchase 30 shares of the Vanguard Target Retirement 2060 Fund, at the price of $34 per share, equating to an overall investment of $1,020.

Additionally, John sets up a monthly contribution with Vanguard, which will automatically purchase $150 worth of shares in this mutual fund on the first day of every month, to be put into his Roth IRA. John is now on his way to saving for his retirement, and if he ever wants to increase or change the amount he is contributing, he can simply log into his Vanguard account and change the amount he contributes with the click of a button.

The beneficial factors of choosing the mutual fund used in the example above is that it is automatically tailored to John's needs as an investor, in accordance with the date he wants to retire. These types of funds help investors manage risk appropriately by selecting stocks and bonds for retirement savings accounts, and by ensuring that the ratio of stocks to bonds in the fund are concurrent with the level of risk that is appropriate for someone retiring in the year of 2060.

Why is the "ratio of stocks to bonds" in a fund or account important? Stocks tend to carry more risk than investment grade bonds, because they can fluctuate significantly over time or due to an event such as a terrorist attack, economic recession, or change in monetary policy by the government. When an investor is young, fluctuations in the stock market do not pose as high of a risk, and can actually be considered as a buying opportunity.

If the market dips down for 5 years during your 30's and then recovers, you didn't really lose anything because you are not using the money in the account until you are over the age of 59 ½ anyways. Years later, you will look at a dip that occurred during your 30's, and view it as a time when you were able to purchase some shares for a cheap price! Therefore, it is usually more beneficial to have more stocks than bonds during your younger investing years; this is because stocks tend to produce higher gains than bonds, and you have enough time before you retire to allow for the market to bounce back.

However, if a large dip in the market or recession occurred the year before an investor planed on retiring, having too much money in stocks could be detrimental to the investor's retirement account. As an investor gets closer to retirement, the ratio of stocks and bonds that are included in their IRA needs to change, in order to properly manage the risk of a downturn in the stock market.

The mutual fund selected in the example above will automatically shift the ratio of stocks and bonds included in the fund as the year of 2060 approaches. For example, in the year of 2020, the ratio of stocks/bonds in the fund may be 80/20, but in the year of 2050, the ratio will have shifted to 25/75 in order to better protect the investor. This type of mutual fund allows for investors who know they need to save, but are not highly experienced in investing, to save for retirement without having to worry about managing different accounts or picking the right stocks and bonds. Additionally, investors do not have to pay trading fees when they would like to rebalance their stock to bond ratio, as the fund manager automatically adjusts this.

The example above is just a single example of a reasonable investment instrument and method that you can use to contribute to your IRA. Keep in mind that you can put as many different mutual funds, stocks, bonds, cash, or other investment instruments inside of your IRA. You can choose more than one type of investment; the IRA is simply the *box* that holds all of your retirement investments. There are funds that mirror the S&P 500, NASDAQ, technology sector, bond markets, international markets, emerging markets, etc. I encourage you to conduct some research online and read about the numerous mutual or index funds available with different financial institutions. Investing in these types of funds are a great way to ensure that you are diversified and correctly managing risk, while also maintaining a professionally managed fund without having to pay a large fee for investment management services for advice.

Lastly, something that you should be aware of when choosing different funds to include in your IRA is the expense ratio. An expense ratio is simply the annual fee that the fund charges shareholders. This fee is usually pretty small, and isn't too noticeable during the earlier years of investing, but can become substantial as your retirement account and amount of money that you have invested in a fund increases. Also, as your investment priorities change, realize that you are able to sell shares of one mutual fund or stock that is in your IRA, and use that money to invest in other opportunities (inside of your IRA of course, so that you don't take from your retirement savings).

The example that is given throughout this chapter is a great way for a young, inexperienced, or passive investor to start saving towards retirement. By selecting a fund that is professionally managed and catered towards your projected retirement date, you can ensure that you are not just shooting in the dark by selecting random stocks or bonds to hold in your IRA, and receive a professionally managed retirement plan without paying the expensive fees of hiring a personal investment broker. Stay the course, invest regularly, and continue to read about the fundamentals of investing for retirement and the stock market.

If you decide that you would like to partake in some speculative investing, here are some guidelines that I suggest you follow. First, before investing in anything that is not for your retirement account, you should have at least $10,000 in an IRA, 3 months of living expenses in a savings account, and zero credit card or high interest debt. Secondly, ensure that you monitor the fees that are associated with trading the stocks that you purchase or trade. Excessive trading will result in your profits being used to pay trading fees, and will take away from your bottom line. Lastly, I recommend that you stay away from "penny stocks" or other get rich quick scams. Most "success stories" that you will read about in regards to penny stocks are not true, or involve the once in a lifetime person who simply got lucky.

Here is an example of how people get scammed with penny stocks: Insiders purchase shares at $0.000019 per share, hire marketing firms to advertise about a "hot stock" until it is pushed to $0.02 per share, the stock raises to $0.05 per share from the momentum and paid advertising, and then the insiders sell until the stock goes down to $0.03 per share. The stock still doesn't look that bad on the outside or to the investor who bought in at $0.02 per share, but look at the percentages that the insiders made from selling their shares until the stock dropped a few cents! If you are going to play in the penny stocks market, realize that you are walking into a casino, and most of the news that you read about a company is inflated marketing.

Overall, saving for retirement is a long road that needs to be met with discipline and consistency. Set up your IRA, choose diversified and risk appropriate funds that have low expense ratios, and invest regularly. Don't expect to get rich over night, but keep your eye on the end goal, and realize that this is something that you may have to depend on for the last 30 years of your life.

It is impossible to touch on all of the areas of investing in a single chapter, or even in a book. However, the basic knowledge contained in this chapter is enough to get you started, and should help you understand a little bit of what is going on when people are discussing the market. Of course understanding the market is important in order for you to save for retirement, but also realize that this knowledge is widely known in the corporate world that you may desire to be a part of in the future, and not knowing anything about it could make people perceive you as ignorant in certain professional settings. Keep reading, learning, and investing; it is all for your future!

# SIX

## ESTABLISHING CREDIT & CREDIT CARDS

When a person reaches the age of 18, they become eligible to apply for credit cards and loans without the signature of a parent. Many young adults approach this new opportunity with very little knowledge or idea of how to begin. The insufficient amount of knowledge surrounding this topic results in people falling on their face right at the starting point of the race we call life. This is not necessarily 100% their fault; some blame also belongs to the individuals and institutions who bear the responsibility of preparing young adults for their financial future, and didn't.

When surveyed, nine out of ten college students stated that the education they received in high school regarding establishing credit, getting a loan, or how a credit score is calculated was subpar or inadequate. All of the people who were surveyed agreed that a semester in high school that was focused on establishing credit, basic investing, and general financial information would have prevented them from making at least one financial mistake early on in their adult life.

Establishing and building your credit score is not something to take lightly, as one simple mistake may prevent you from being able to purchase a car, rent an apartment, sign up for household utilities, or qualify for a credit card in the years to come. Although this step in life can carry so many long term consequences, most young adults press head first into this stage of their life with very little understanding of how it is going to affect them in the future, what they qualify for, or how their credit score is even calculated.

Let's fix this problem right now! In this chapter, we are going to cover what a credit score is, how it is calculated, what a score means, the proper way to establish and build credit, and things to avoid while going through this process so that you don't damage your credit early on.

First, let's begin with gaining an understanding of what a credit score is and the details of how it is calculated. The actual name for the score that you may be familiar with is called a FICO score. This simply stands for Fair Isaac Corporation, which is the name of an analytics company that was founded in 1956, and has become widely relied upon for the production and creation of consumer credit scores. The FICO score is the most trusted credit scoring system by major financial and lending institutions across the United States.

When a FICO score is calculated, weighted categories are added together in order to produce a number that ranges from 300 to 850, with 300 representing extremely bad credit and 850 representing perfect credit. The categories that are evaluated while calculating a FICO score are payment history, amount owed, length of credit history, credit mix, and new credit. Each category represents a certain percentage of your score, meaning that the categories carry a different amount of weight when your overall score is created.

Your payment history is the most important category when determining your score, because it is weighted at 35% of your FICO score. Realize that the reason lenders and creditors check your credit score, or even care about it at all, is because it helps them evaluate the level of risk that they are accepting by lending you money.

Regardless of what stage you are at in the credit building process, it is extremely important that you always pay your bills on time, as this is the heaviest determining factor in the calculation of your FICO score, and negative incidents will result in dramatic changes that will have an adverse effect on your score for years to come. Understand that any missed or late payments will remain on your credit report for future lenders to see; this period can be as long as seven years from the date that the debt became delinquent.

The next category that is evaluated when calculating your FICO score is amount owed. This category refers to the amount of debt that you have in comparison to your credit limits, and accounts for 30% of your FICO score. Carrying a small amount of debt, let's say 15% of your credit limit, does not necessarily mean that you should be labeled as high risk and assigned a low credit score (even though I will always advise against carrying any debt that you have to pay interest on).

Significant problems arise in the "amount owed" category when consumers hover around their credit limit, or come close to being maxed out. If a person has a credit card with a $5,000 limit, and they are carrying a balance of $4,850, this simply shows future creditors that they are overextending themselves, and are more likely to default on their debts. Creditors like to see responsible spending, and are more likely to lend to people who don't have to rely upon their credit cards or loans to make it from one pay period to the next.

A good rule to follow regarding the amount owed category is to never allow the balance of your credit cards to reach higher than 30% of your credit limit. This threshold should be viewed by you as your maximum credit limit, and an amount that you should never exceed if you are focused on building a higher FICO score. Anything higher than 30% will send a signal to future lenders that you need your credit cards to survive with the amount of debt that you currently have, so giving you more debt would be foolish and will come as a higher risk to them.

Lastly, consumers with a lower amount of debt, and more available credit are favored by lenders because they have some "wiggle room" to handle unexpected events or emergencies. For instance, if your car breaks down unexpectedly and you do not have the cash to fix it, you are more likely to put some other expenses on your credit card while making repairs to your vehicle than you are to miss a payment that will have an adverse affect on your credit score; this is something that someone with maxed out credit cards cannot do, which could result in them missing payments on other debts.

The length of your credit history is also a determining factor in calculating your credit score. This category represents 15% of your FICO score and simply takes time to increase, since time is precisely what this category measures. Simply put, people who do not have a long history of paying their bills on time carry a higher risk than those with an established credit history. This will be frustrating for young adults who are meticulously trying to raise their credit score by taking all of the right steps, but the truth is that sometimes you just have to prove yourself over time to gain trust.

The best thing that you can do to increase your score in this category is to always pay your bills on time, and to avoid frequently starting new lines of credit that will lower the average amount of years that you have had credit established. Lastly, keep old accounts that do not charge an annual fee open in order to increase the average amount of years that you have had credit established for.

Next, the type of debt that you carry will have some affect on your overall FICO score. The "credit mix" category makes up 10% of your FICO score and helps lenders see what kind of debt you have. This is something that lenders look at because $30,000 of debt that is for a family vehicle, and $30,000 of credit card debt are two very different things.

Although this category does not make up a large percentage of your FICO score, it is important to monitor what type of debt that you carry. Stay away from retail store credit cards. Signing up for one of these types of cards simply shows creditors that you may not be able to afford everyday items without your credit card; these cards also carry some of the highest interest rates, usually around the 28% mark. To be clear, I am not stating that having one retail store card is going to ruin your credit or severely lower your score, but that you need to ensure that these types of cards or debt does not monopolize the type of debt that you carry.

The last category that is used to calculate your score is "new credit", and it also accounts for 10% of your FICO score. The new credit category looks at how many accounts have been added to your credit report over a recent period of time. Consumers who open numerous accounts over a short period of time are considered to carry a higher amount of risk; therefore, opening multiple accounts in a short period of time will lower your FICO score.

Additionally, shopping or applying for credit at multiple locations may have a negative impact on your score, especially if you are consistently getting denied. A hard inquiry occurs when a creditor requests your credit report, for the purpose of approving a loan or line of credit. Too many hard inquiries can result in lowering your FICO score. Additionally, if you are denied credit by multiple lenders, it raises the question to other lenders of why they would want to give you money when others didn't.

The FICO scoring system understands that people need to apply for credit in order to establish and maintain it; therefore the penalty for doing so is usually minimal. Also, it is understood that consumers may submit multiple applications for credit to simply see which lender is going to give them the best interest rate, which is not what causes a problem or lowers a consumer's score. The problem in this category occurs when a consumer applies for credit excessively, and when multiple denials for credit occur over a short and recent period of time.

Overall, try to refrain from signing up for multiple lines of credit or credit cards during a short period of time, and limit the amount of hard inquiries present on your report.

The categories that we just discussed are combined, in accordance with their weighted percentage, and your FICO score is created. Earlier in this chapter, we covered that the FICO score ranges from 300 to 850.

The FICO score that you receive is also broken down into categories, such as bad, poor, fair, good, and excellent. Example 6.1 shows what category a consumer will fall into based on their FICO score.

Example 6.1

| Category | FICO Score (Range) |
|----------|--------------------|
| Excellent | Above 750 |
| Good | 700-749 |
| Fair | 650-699 |
| Poor | 550-649 |
| Bad | Below 550 |

Now that we have covered what a score is, how it is calculated, and the categories associated with a score, let's dive into productive ways for you to establish and build credit.

The process of establishing your credit is one that needs to be embarked upon carefully and intentionally. Starting off the process of establishing your credit on the wrong foot can result in years of negative consequences. Unfortunately, most young adults head in the wrong direction when initially trying to establish their credit, because they have never been instructed on the proper way to do so.

Running to the nearest shopping mall and applying for a credit card at all of the popular retail stores is a big mistake, but is usually what happens, and is a very common way that eighteen to twenty year olds try to establish their credit. Do not fall into this very common mistake of young adults by putting this type of blemish on your credit report early on!

Let's discuss three different ways that you can establish and start building your credit, without the risk of placing multiple hard inquiries and denials on your credit report. These methods can all be started as early as the age of eighteen, and will get you headed in the right direction early on in life.

The first step that someone should take in order to establish credit is to open a secured credit card. A secured credit card is different from a regular (or unsecured) credit card because it requires the card holder to make a cash deposit, that becomes the line of credit, or limit associated with the card. For instance, if a consumer deposits $300 into the account that is associated with the secured card, their spending limit for that card will be $300.

Secured credit cards are easy for consumers with zero credit history or bad credit to obtain because the card issuer is not assuming any of the risk, and can only gain from the deal. Unlike traditional credit cards, that essentially loan consumers money with the risk of not being paid back, consumers with secured cards are only able to spend up to the amount of money deposited as collateral, and the card issuer can automatically recoup their money if payments are not made on time.

Opening a secured credit card benefits consumers who are establishing and trying to increase their credit score for a few different reasons. First, on time payments are reported to credit agencies; therefore, the payments that are made will help the card user establish a credit timeline and payment history. Also, the money that is deposited as collateral for the secured card is usually placed into an interest bearing account by the card issuer, which the card holder gets to benefit from.

Lastly, if the card holder of a secure card misses a payment, the collateral will be used to pay off the debt; this prevents the debt from being forwarded to a debt collector, and the harassment that is sure to stem from not paying the bill. Understand that this does not mean that missed or late payments are not reported to credit reporting agencies, just that the collateral is automatically used to pay the late payment instead of the user being hunted down by a debt collector. If payments on secured cards are missed or made after the due date, it will be reported and will have a negative effect on the card holder's FICO score.

There are some downsides or drawbacks associated with having one of these cards, but they are minimal for someone trying to establish credit for the first time. The first drawback is that the applicant has to part ways with the initial deposit that is required to open the account. Additionally, interest rates for carrying a balance on these cards tend to be very high, and card holders usually have to pay application, processing, and annual fees in order to sign up for the card.

For card users who are establishing or rebuilding their credit, the benefits of secured cards far outweigh the drawbacks. Secured card holders should ensure that all payments are made on time, and that the full balance on the card is paid off completely each month to avoid interest charges.

Another way that young adults are able to establish credit is by being added as an authorized user on a parent's credit card. When you are added as an authorized user, you will not be able to request increases in credit limits or make changes to the account, but you will be issued a card in your name, and the payments that are made on the account will count towards your score and credit history.

When being added to a credit card as an authorized user, it is extremely important that you fully understand that this can negatively affect your score as well. Although the account holder is the one who is ultimately responsible for paying the debt on the card, missed or late payments will be reported on an authorized user's credit report as well.

Being added as an authorized user should only be considered as an option if you are absolutely certain that the bill is going to be paid on time every month. This method is usually used by someone who has parents with good credit, and always pays their bills on time. I strongly suggest avoiding this option if you have to rely upon a friend, someone who has debt that surpasses 30% of their credit limit, or someone with a history of not paying their bills on time. Also, make sure to speak with the credit card company prior to being added as an authorized user to ensure that their policy is to report authorized users to the credit reporting bureaus, as some credit card companies do not.

The last method that we are going to discuss in regards to establishing credit is co-signing. Co-signing can help a person with zero credit history qualify for a loan or line of credit that they would not normally qualify for on their own.

For instance, if you are attempting to purchase a vehicle and have zero credit history, the likelihood of getting approved for a loan is very low. However, if a family member who has a good credit score agrees to co-sign the loan with you, the chances of getting approved increase significantly and you will likely qualify for a lower interest rate. When completed properly, co-signing prevents a person with zero credit from paying higher interest rates, or not qualifying for the loan all together.

Understand that the primary loan holder is ultimately responsible for the debt, but that the loan and payments will appear on both peoples' credit report. Realize that if payments are not made on time, both parties associated with the loan will have adverse marks entered on their credit report. The person who is considered as the primary on the loan will be held responsible for making payments and any late fees if the loan is not paid on time. If someone is generous enough to co-sign a form of debt for you, ensure that you show your appreciation by making payments on time!

Now that we have covered ways to properly establish credit, let's go over some things to avoid when going through this process. First, do not apply for a loan or card that you are not likely to be approved for, or offers that seem too good to be true. Realize that some companies will target younger people in an attempt to take advantage of them early on. Offers that people with zero credit history usually receive in the mail for personal loans or credit cards tend come with enormous interest rates, multiple stipulations, and large annual fees. It is best to speak directly to the bank that you use for your checking or savings accounts when establishing your credit to see what offers best fit your current financial circumstances.

Avoid "rent payment" reporting services. These are companies that sell you on the idea that you can build your credit history through the use of their services when you pay your rent every month. Instead of paying your rent directly to a property management company or home owner, you will pay the company, and they will pay your rent for you.

The company reports this information to the credit reporting bureaus, and the payments that you make are annotated on your credit report. Although these types of companies can do what they claim, this type of service comes with a charge or fee; it is my opinion that the additional amount of money that you are paying to have a rent payment reported to the credit agencies each month is not worth the few points you will gain on your score.

Also, beware of the companies that sell "credit repair" or "credit building" services. Stay far away! You do not need to pay a company to establish or fix your credit; simply use the methods discussed earlier in this chapter, and save or invest the money that these companies would have charged you for their services.

The last area involving credit and credit scores that we are going to cover in this chapter is monitoring your credit report. You are entitled to receive one free credit report per year from each of the three credit reporting agencies, which are Equifax, Experian, and TransUnion. To receive a free copy of your credit report, visit www.annualcreditreport.com. This site will allow you to view your report with each reporting agency to ensure that your report is accurate.

If you have an item on your credit report that you would like to dispute, you can do so on your own, and at no cost by submitting a claim with Equifax, Experian, or TransUnion. These credit reporting agencies have simple to follow instructions on their websites, and have people manning a help desk who can help you through the process of removing an error on your credit report. There is no reason to pay anyone for this service, and it is highly recommended that you check your report for accuracy on an annual basis.

# SEVEN

## UNDERSTANDING YOUR TAXES

There are very few things in the world that are more confusing than the American tax system. Many Americans receive their paycheck, and are left scratching their head or wondering why so much money was deducted from their check by the government.

Here are some common questions asked by young adults every day: What credits or deductions do I qualify for? Where do I get a W-2 from? What is an "allowance" and how many should I list on my

W-4? Should I hire an accountant to prepare my annual tax return? Should I choose the itemized or standard deduction?

One of the most common statements that I have heard regarding the public education system is "I learned a bunch of stuff in school that I never use, but I didn't learn how to do my taxes, apply for a job, invest, or create a budget". We have covered most of these areas throughout the previous chapters in this book, and now it is time to dive into understanding your taxes.

Let's start at the beginning with the first tax form that you will have to complete upon getting hired at a job, which is called a W-4. A W-4 form is used by an employer to determine the proper amount of income tax to withhold from an employee's paycheck. Employees are required to fill out a W-4 upon starting a job, and I recommend reviewing it each year to ensure that the form still represents your circumstances accurately. It is also important to fill out a new W-4 anytime your circumstances change, such as when you get married, have children, or there is a significant change in the amount of money you make.

The most important choice that you are going to have to make when completing a W-4 is selecting the amount of "allowances" that you are going to claim; this is widely referred to as the number of dependents that you are wishing to claim. Most employees who are not married and do not have any children, input a zero in this field to ensure that they are not going to owe the government any taxes at the end of the year.

By claiming zero allowances, your employer is going to withhold the maximum amount of income taxes from your paycheck each month; this will result in you receiving a smaller paycheck each month, but a larger income tax return at the end of the year when you file your taxes. If you decide to increase the number of allowances that you would like to claim, your paycheck will increase, but be aware that you will receive a smaller refund check, or may even have to pay some taxes at the end of the year.

If you are single, and do not have any deductions that you can claim in order to lower the amount of taxes that you are responsible for paying each year, I highly recommend never inputting a number higher than two on this form, as it will likely result in you having to write a check at the end of the year.

The intelligent decision regarding the number of allowances that you claim is to aim for not getting a refund, and also owing zero at the end of the year. This way, you are able to invest or save the additional money throughout the year in an interest bearing account, instead of letting the government hold onto money that you could be profiting from.

The next important form in regards to your taxes is the W-2 form. This form is sent to you by your employer at the end of the year, and is used to report how much income that you made in the form of wages, tips, or other types of compensation such as a bonus or commission. Federal law requires all employers to provide their employees with a W-2 no later than January 31st of the next year; this affords employees the opportunity to gather all required documents and file their taxes before the identified deadline, which is April 15th or the next business day if that date happens to fall on a weekend or special event.

All income that is received during the year is considered taxable. It is your responsibility to report any tips or other compensation that you receive throughout the year. Also, it is your responsibility to update prior employers of changes to your address and contact information, so that they can send your W-2 to the correct location at the end of the year.

Although a W-2 reports all of the income that you received from your employer, realize that you may have income that was generated from other assets or locations, such as your savings account or investment funds. If you have money in a savings account, and made interest from that money, this is considered taxable income and you need to ensure that you receive a 1099-INT. The financial institution where your savings account is located at will provide you with this form, or may send you instructions for how to download it using your online account.

Before attempting to file your taxes at the end of the year, ensure that you have received all of the appropriate tax forms from any account where you keep money at, or anywhere that withheld taxes from you throughout the year. Other places that might send you a tax form may include the financial institution that holds your student loans, the state in which you are a resident of, or an investment broker.

Once you are sure that you received all of your tax forms, it is time to start looking for deductions or credits that you may qualify for. Deductions allow the taxpayer to "deduct" a specific amount of their income from the amount that is considered as taxable income.

A credit is simply money that offsets the amount of taxes that you owe. With a tax deduction, if a person falls into the 20% tax bracket and receives a $2,000 deduction, the amount that they will have to pay in taxes is lowered by $400. A credit benefits a taxpayer by simply reducing the amount of tax owed, in accordance with the amount of the credit; therefore, if a person owes $3,000 in taxes, but receives a $500 credit, the amount of taxes that they owe is reduced to $2,500.

There are too many types of deductions and credits available to cover every one in a single chapter, but let's go over some of the most common ones, and highlight the deductions and credits that are most popular for the age demographic that this book has been written for.

First, let's start with the decision to select a "standard" or "itemized" deduction when filing your taxes. A standard deduction is designed for taxpayers who do not have a large amount of work related expenses, such as purchasing uniform items, using a personal vehicle for work purposes, or buying an excessive amount of items that are necessary for employment. The amount of the deduction that you receive will depend on your filing status, which is shown on the chart in example 7.1 (2017 Tax Year).

Example 7.1

| Filing Status | Standard Deduction |
|---|---|
| Single | $6,350 |
| Married-Joint | $12,700 |
| Married-Separate | $6,350 |
| Head of Household | $9,350 |

In order to decide if the standard deduction is the best decision for you, you will need to evaluate the amount of deductible expenses that you have. If your expenses for the year do not exceed the amount of the standard deduction that is associated with your filing status, then it is more beneficial for you to select a standard deduction. If your deductible expenses exceed the amount of the standard deduction, and you have the documentation to prove it, then you will benefit more from itemizing your deductions when filing your return.

Some common items other than work expenses that may qualify as deductions are: Home mortgage interest, real estate taxes, brokerage or investing fees, medical expenses, charitable contributions, and qualifying educational expenses. If you decide that it is more beneficial for you to select the itemized deduction, you will need to use a separate form called a "Schedule-A" to list your deductions, and complete your taxes using an IRS Form 1040.

Tax credits that are common for young adults to receive when filing their taxes are the earned income credit, saver's credit, education credit, and child tax credit. I recommend visiting the IRS's website when starting to prepare your taxes to look through the entire list of credits that are available to ensure that you do not miss any that you qualify for.

The Earned-Income Credit (EIC) was designed to provide financial relief to taxpayers in low-income categories. The credit that a taxpayer receives is determined by factors such as their income and the number of qualified dependents they are able to claim. In the year of 2016, taxpayers who filed as "single" and earned less than $47,955 may have qualified for a credit up to $6,269 depending on the amount of dependents they are able to claim. A single taxpayer with no dependents, who earned less than $14,880 qualified for a credit as high as $506. Maximum income requirements are significantly different for taxpayers who file as married, because both people's income is factored into the amount.

The saver's credit, formally known as the Retirement Savings Contributions Credit, was implemented into the tax code to reward low and middle income taxpayers who are saving for retirement. This credit is widely overlooked by young investors, which is unfortunate since it rewards people with money, for saving money!

The requirements to qualify for this credit depend on the taxpayer's filing status and adjusted gross income (income minus deductions). In 2017, single taxpayers with an adjusted gross income lower than $30,750 qualified for a credit as high as 50% of the amount of money they invested into qualifying accounts, up to the amount of $2,000. For example, if a taxpayer contributed $2,000 into their IRA, and did not exceed the maximum adjusted gross income level for their filing status, they will receive a credit of $1,000. This is $1,000 that the government is giving you, for saving $2,000; that's hard to beat, and something that I am sure a majority of people wish they would have known about earlier in life!

Taxpayers who have expenses related to higher education may also qualify for a tax credit. There are currently two types of education credits, which are the American Opportunity Credit and Lifetime Learning Credit. The qualifications for these credits are associated with the taxpayer's adjusted gross income and filing status, but also have requirements surrounding student enrollment status.

For the filing year of 2017, eligible tax payers are able to receive a maximum credit of $2,500 with the American Opportunity Credit and up to $2,000 with the Lifetime Learning Credit. The value of these credits is calculated by using a percentage of qualified expenses; for instance, a $2,000 credit can be rewarded with the Lifetime Learning Credit when a taxpayer spends $10,000 throughout the year on qualified expenses, because the credit will give the taxpayer up to 20% of the first $10,000 back in the form of a credit.

Specifics to qualify for educational credits change annually, therefore it is in your best interest to visit the IRS's website while preparing your taxes if you were a student during the year that you are preparing taxes for. A taxpayer will only receive this credit if they have qualifying educational expenses. A qualifying expense is identified as items such as tuition, course-related books or materials, lab fees, supplies, or costs associated with participating in student activities.

The last credit that we are going to discuss is the Child Tax Credit; this credit is only applicable to taxpayers who have children under the age of 17, and are eligible to be claimed as a dependent on a parent's income tax filing. Simply put, the government realizes that children are an added expense, and offers a credit to offset some of the costs that are associated with raising a child.

The value of the credit per child is $1,000; this amount is scheduled to be increased to $2,000 per child in the year of 2018. To qualify for this credit, the child must be a legal resident, reside with the taxpayer for a period longer than half of the tax year, and cannot be responsible for providing more than half of their own support.

After reviewing your income, deductions, and credits, it is time to file your annual tax return. Unless you are in a situation that requires you to itemize your deductions, you own a business, or you have a complex financial situation, filing your taxes without paying a professional is easy, and can be completed within a few hours. Hiring a company to prepare your taxes is costly, and usually unnecessary.

Most young adults will save money when filing their own taxes by using a free program or affordable online service. These sites offer professional assistance, and are advanced enough to check through your tax filing to see if you missed any credits that you qualify for. If you are smart enough to read this book, you are smart enough to file your own taxes!

Made in the USA
Monee, IL
11 June 2020